Mastering Attachment Theory

Practical Techniques for Transforming Attachment Styles & Building Healthy Relationships

PUBLISHED BY: Stanley Sheppard

Copyright _____ **2023 - All rights reserved.**

The content contained within this book may not be reproduced, duplicated or transmitted without direct written permission from the author or the publisher.

Under no circumstances will any blame or legal responsibility be held against the publisher, or author, for any damages, reparation, or monetary loss due to the information contained within this book. Either directly or indirectly. You are responsible for your own choices, actions, and results.

Legal Notice:

This book is copyright protected. This book is only for personal use. You cannot amend, distribute, sell, use, quote or paraphrase any part, or the content within this book, without the consent of the author or publisher.

Disclaimer Notice:

Please note the information contained within this document is for educational and entertainment purposes only. All effort has been executed to present accurate, up to date, and reliable, complete information. No warranties of any kind are declared or implied. Readers acknowledge that the author is not engaging in the rendering of legal, financial, medical or professional advice.

By reading this document, the reader agrees that under no circumstances is the author responsible for any losses, direct or indirect, which are incurred as a result of the use of the information contained within this document, including, but not limited to, — errors, omissions, or inaccuracies.

Table of Contents

Understanding Attachment Theory 1
    Types of Attachment Styles: 1
    The Importance of Attachment Styles 8
    Different Attachment Styles in Adult Relationships 10

The Mind-Body Connection 18
    So What Is The Mind-Body Connection? 18
    Body Maps of Emotions 20
    How the Mind-Body Connection Relates to Attachment 22
    Emotions Turning Physical 24
    Techniques for Cultivating Mindfulness and Body Awareness 25

Healing Attachment Wounds 38
    Recognizing and Understanding Attachment-Related Wounds ... 38
    Importance of Self-Compassion And Self-Care In Healing 40
    Exercises and Techniques for Healing Past Attachment Wounds 42

Developing Authentic Connections 55
    Exploration of Authentic Connections in Relationships: 56
    Understanding and Overcoming Barriers to Authenticity: 60
    Practical Exercises for Fostering Authentic Connections
    with Others: 64

Integrating Mindfulness and Somatic Practices 71
    Mindfulness Practices and Their Role in Attachment
    Transformation 71
    Mindfulness and Somatic Practices You Can Use 73
    Incorporating Somatic Techniques to Deepen Self-Awareness and
    Regulation 76

    How Exactly Do Somatic Techniques Help Deepen Self-Awareness and Emotional Regulation? 78

    Mindfulness And Somatic Exercises for Enhancing Attachment Security 82

    R.A.I.N 82

        Somatic Exercises 86

        Breathing exercises 86

        Mindful communication 86

        Self-compassion 87

Nurturing Self-Compassion 91

    Importance of Self-Compassion in Building Healthy Relationships: 92

    Techniques for Cultivating Self-Compassion and Self-Acceptance:.. 96

    Self-Reflective Exercises for Developing Self-Compassion in Attachment Relationships 100

Enhancing Relationship Skills 107

    Effective Communication Strategies for Building Secure Attachments: 107

    Conflict Resolution Techniques for Healthier Relationship Dynamics 113

    Practical Exercises for Improving Relationship Skills 116

Cultivating Growth and Transformation 121

    Embracing Personal Growth and Development Through Attachment Transformation 121

    Long-Term Strategies for Maintaining Healthy Attachments 126

    Here are some tips and exercises to help you develop this skill: 129

    Tools for Integrating Newfound Knowledge into Everyday Life... 132

Conclusion 137

References 141

Your Free Bonus

As a way of saying thanks for your purchase, I'm offering these FOUR books for FREE to my readers. To get instant access just go to: https://greatlifebooks.com/CBT-Workbook-free-bonus

- ❖ **CBT for Procrastination Workbook**: How to overcome procrastination, boost productivity, and take control of your life

- ❖ **8 Highly Effective Ways to Relieve Stress**: The ultimate guide to stress management

- ❖ **Overcome Anxiety**: How to stop the cycle of anxiety, worry and fear so you can regain control of your life

- ❖ **Resilience**: How to build mental strength to overcome any difficult situation and live a better life

Don't let stress control your life any longer. Take charge and discover the secrets to a calmer, more enjoyable existence. Download these free books now and start your transformation today!

Understanding Attachment Theory

"Attachment is the deep and lasting imprint that connects us to others and influences how we relate to love and experience the world." - Unknown.

Picture this: as a little bundle of joy, you are starting to explore the world around you. But wait, there's something you need first—a trusty caregiver! Attachment theory tells us that as babies, we instinctively crave that special bond with our primary caretakers, usually mom or dad (or maybe a loving aunt or uncle!).

The attachment theory sheds light on relationships and connections (especially long-term ones) between individuals. This could be the bond between a parent and a child or between two romantic partners. It is the Psychological Lingo for emotional bonds between people.

But where did the term' Attachment Theory' even come from? Well, a British Psychologist named John Bowlby spent his days observing children who had been separated from their caregivers and he realized these children were experiencing tons of stress and anxiety. He claimed that children need secure attachment and coined the Attachment Theory Itself.

This theory tells us that humans are born with an innate need to form bonds with those who care for them and that these connections continue to play vital roles in our lives as we grow older.

Types of Attachment Styles:

Depending on the bond we develop with our caregiver, we can have different attachment styles. Let's meet the crew:

- **Secure Attachment**

    These lucky ducks have hit the jackpot! They feel safe, loved, and super cozy with their caregivers. They know their caregiver will be there when they need a hug or help. As they grow up, securely attached folks usually have super healthy relationships. This is primarily because they have had a solid foundation built on trust and love.

    Fun fact: Researchers examined the relationship between secure attachment styles and resilience in a 2018 publication from the Journal Personality and Social Psychology Bulletin. For half a year, the study followed the journey of 200 participants. It concluded that those with secure attachment styles were more adept at managing stress and overcoming difficulties optimally.

    Check it out:

    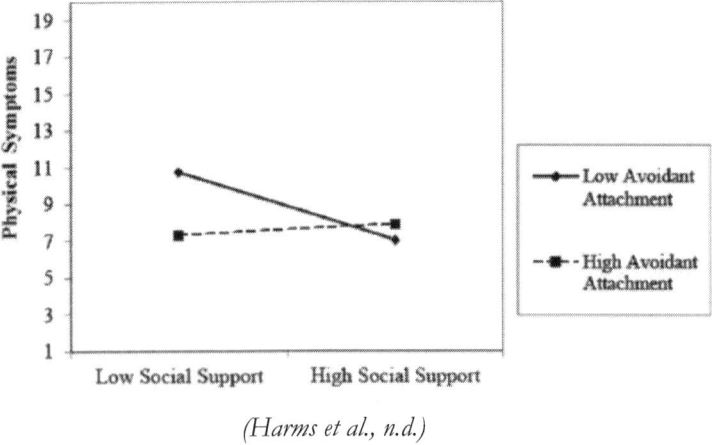

    (Harms et al., n.d.)

    Securely attached individuals can feel safe, loved, and oh-so-cozy with their caregivers. For them, it feels like being engulfed in a comforting and loving embrace from those who care for them. They instinctively know that their caregiver will always have their back if they require assistance, be it an attentive ear or support with any task.

But here's the cool part: this solid foundation of trust and love sets the stage for some seriously healthy relationships as you grow up. Securely attached folks have a leg up in the relationship game. They've got the skills to create deep, meaningful connections with others.

Because you've experienced consistent love and support from your caregivers, you learn to trust that others can provide the same. This trust becomes the magical ingredient in your relationship recipe. Knowing you're worthy of love and care allows you to be open, vulnerable, and authentic with others.

Secure attachment gives you a head start regarding communication and emotional intimacy. Your caregiver's example taught you to engage in responsive and meaningful interactions. You've had plenty of practice in expressing your needs, listening attentively, and understanding the feelings of others. These skills become your secret weapon in building and maintaining healthy relationships.

Your secure attachment experience also shapes your expectations in relationships. Having been accustomed to receiving appreciation, benevolence, and encouragement in your relationships, it's natural for you to desire the same qualities in potential love interests and companions. You hold yourself and others to high standards, but that doesn't mean you're overbearing. Instead, it is a means of providing an environment where kindness and affection can thrive.

Securely attached individuals tend to have a solid sense of self-worth. A strong sense of self-worth and confidence is vital in any healthy relationship! It ensures you establish boundaries, express your thoughts effectively, and advocate for yourself gracefully in all situations. An added benefit of cultivating positive self-worth is that it lets you enter partnerships as an equal competitor who can respectfully meet the needs of others while ensuring those critical goals are met for themselves too. No beating around the bush with these guys!

- **Anxious-Preoccupied Attachment:**

Ah, the worrywarts of the attachment world. This bunch often feels uncertain about their caregiver's attention. They might constantly seek reassurance and need to be glued to their caretakers. As they grow up, they may have self-esteem issues and crave external validation to feel fulfilled.

Our attachment patterns can profoundly affect our relationships and self-image as we grow up. Imagine being an anxious-preoccupied individual constantly questioning their worth, seeking validation from others, and trying to read the most minor signs of love or approval. This can make you feel constantly on edge, worried about rejection or abandonment, distrustful of others, and unable to form secure connections.

The result is a turbulent ride that causes one's sense of security and stability to suffer greatly. Remembering the inner critic voice isn't easy either; it whispers self-doubt into your ear all too often! You tend to readily seek external validation for affirmation of being worthwhile when relying solely on yourself will do you wonders.

By understanding your anxious-preoccupied tendencies, you can work on building your self-esteem from within. Learning to trust and love yourself, independent of others' opinions, can be a game-changer. It's like embracing your worthiness, knowing you don't need constant external validation to feel fulfilled.

Building secure and healthy relationships may take extra effort for you. Communicating your needs and fears to your partners is essential, allowing them to understand and support you. Developing trust and establishing secure connections may require patience and open communication, but it's impossible.

- **Avoidant Attachment:**

    Meet the little independent wanderers! These mini-explorers prefer to go solo and keep their distance from their caregivers. They might seem self-reliant and not too keen on seeking emotional support. As they grow up, they may find it very hard to get close to others and may even develop a fear of being open or becoming too vulnerable.

    You're one of these independent wanderers. You like being independent and enjoy facing challenges all by yourself. The concept of wanting emotional support might not be essential to you. It's almost as if you foster this personal sanctuary of autonomy, where it's more comfortable to venture out into the world without excessive dependence on others.

These connection patterns can affect how well you make friends when you get older. It's like creating an unseen shield around your heart, making it hard to allow others inside. Opening up to others and sharing our emotions can be awkward and scary sometimes.

You might have difficulty telling people what you want and how you feel because you're worried it could make you weak or needy. You've gotten good at keeping away to avoid getting hurt by depending on others. Feeling uneasy can happen when you get too close to someone because independence becomes your usual way.

This trait of being emotionally independent might cause problems when trying to establish meaningful and close relationships. You might still want love and someone beside you, but a part inside is unsure about fully committing. Because of this internal battle, you might feel different emotions about being close to others in relationships. I hope to connect with others, but I also Communicating getting too close.

Don't worry; I've got your back. You can build safe and happy relationships! Knowing your attachment style is the initial step in making good changes.

Understanding what patterns mean and knowing your emotional needs are very important. Finding a balance between personal freedom and the natural desire for connections is essential. To make better friendships, talking well, showing feelings truthfully and bravely, and trying new things by trusting others are crucial. Doing this takes purposeful work but, in the end, leads to more robust and rewarding connections. Finding a patient and empathetic partner is essential. This person must give you ample space and time to grow comfortable in their presence. Over time, stepping beyond your comfort zone can develop a sense of trust and closeness.

Allowing yourself to be vulnerable can be pretty scary, but it leads to forming better emotional bonds. Sharing your innermost thoughts with people you love and trust helps you become more open and foster trusted connections. It is important to remember that vulnerability isn't a weakness but a strength that will only help you grow.

- **Disorganized Attachment:**

    Here's the thing: folks with disorganized attachments are a bag of mixed emotions! They have extreme highs and lows of emotions with their loved ones—sometimes, they want to run into their arms, while other times, they feel frightened or flustered. As adults, they might find it challenging to regulate their emotions or maintain stable relationships.

    Imagine being one of these individuals. Imagine a tumultuous maelstrom of emotions simultaneously pulling you towards your loved ones with an overwhelming desire for connection while pushing you away in fear and confusion. These interconnected feelings can be overwhelmingly intense at times.

    As grown-ups with disorganized attachment patterns, these emotional storms can challenge regulating emotions, leading to difficulty in forming stable relationships. It's like trying to find that sweet spot of emotional balance and navigating love and intimacy.

You might struggle with keeping your emotions in check, experiencing these wild mood swings, or feeling totally swamped by conflicting feelings. It's almost similar to being tangled up in tumultuous emotions, not comprehending how to quell the brewing tempest within yourself. This predicament can cause difficulty when trying to maintain emotional equanimity in relationships and often leads to significant fluctuations in feelings.

The Importance of Attachment Styles

Why is understanding the attachment theory so important?

Attachment styles are essential for how we connect with others and experience love. They're like the special ingredient that affects how we build connections and explore the unpredictable realm of feelings.

Attachment, essentially, comes from feeling safe, secure, and loved. It protects your heart like a nice, snug blanket. Having solid bonds helps us feel safe and gives us the courage to face life's difficulties confidently.

Attachment starts shaping our lives as soon as we're born. This invisible force shapes our first relationships, especially with our caregivers. As children, we depend on our adults to care for us and meet all our bodily or emotional requirements. It's like a unique mix for creating a solid connection when they always answer us affectionately.

Having a secure attachment is just like having a superpower! How we are raised as kids affects how we interact with others and see ourselves later. We feel important and dependent on others when we are safe and loved during adolescence. We grow up understanding love and trust others because of it.

Interestingly, the strong bonds we form as kids can impact our adult relationships too! When we have felt loved and supported initially, it is as if we build a strong base of trust that continues into our relationships and friendships.

Adults who are securely attached generally have better relationships. It's similar to how they have this natural feeling of safety and belief that lets them show vulnerability, be open, and have emotions. They can easily communicate their needs, express their feelings, and deal with conflicts. They have a perfect set of tools to make and keep loving relationships.

But we should remember the other attachment styles. Some people might feel worried and cling to others, wanting them to reassure and being afraid they will be rejected. Feels like having a caring heart wanting acknowledgment and companionship. They might require additional assistance and comprehension to feel safe in their connections.

Now we must pay some heed to our friends with avoidant attachment styles. They like being independent and relying on themselves and enjoy the freedom to explore relationships. But at times, it can be daunting for them to fully start sharing their true self and allow others to join in.

Lastly, disorganized attachment can feel like the ups and downs of a rollercoaster ride - one moment elated with love, then suddenly fraught with fear and confusion. For those grappling with these complex emotions, actively cultivating self-awareness and seeking guidance from mental health professionals can help ease the tumultuous journey.

Different Attachment Styles in Adult Relationships

You may have never really taken the time to deeply reflect on or analyze your actions within relationships. However, you may have noticed recurring patterns in your love life.

Have you ever questioned why you are in similar situations, even though the partners may change? Do you tend to become overly clingy or jealous? Or do you consistently find yourself more invested in the relationship than your partner? Maybe you desire a connection with someone, but once things become emotionally intimate, you instinctively pull away.

If you've observed a pattern of unhealthy and emotionally challenging behaviors in your romantic experiences, it could be worthwhile to delve into how you form attachments in intimate relationships. Understanding attachment theory can be valuable.

- **Secure Attachment Style - The healthy lovers**

    Meet Martha and Ed. They have been married for 5 years now and enjoy spending time with each other just as much as they did the first time they met. But what's interesting is that Martha and Ed have jobs requiring lots of travel and significant time apart. So how do these two people maintain such a healthy relationship? Well, because they are securely attached!

    Individuals with a secure attachment style are comfortable expressing their emotions openly and honestly. Trust and comfort in connecting with others enable them to grow healthy partnerships where both parties can entirely rely on each other. Within secure attachments are fundamental components such as emotional closeness and tolerance. These aspects become the bedrock of genuine relationships created for open communication without fear of judgment or dismissal.

The most remarkable feature about those who have developed this style is that they maintain independence while thriving within their bond - talk about the best of both worlds! They do not depend wholly on approval or responsiveness from partners for self-worth or personal happiness. Instead, they have healthy self-assurance and positivity towards themselves, their environment, and others around them.

Balanced interactions thrive in individuals who value partnership while embracing their autonomy fully. Individuals adopting this approach understand that theirs will be an authentic pairing founded upon equally meaningful associations with mutual validation instead of emotional dependency alone to attain happiness.

- **Anxious-Preoccupied Attachment style - The Insecure lovers**

    Ever heard of the clingy boyfriend or the girlfriend who keeps asking you if you would still love her if she was a worm? Well, that's where Sarah and Tom come in. They're both constantly asking each other for validation and feel super insecure when the other isn't around. That is simply the result of an anxious-preoccupied attachment style.

When adults have an anxious attachment style, their partner often becomes their "better half" and provides stability during life's challenges. Living without their partner or being alone can make their anxiety skyrocket. People who have this attachment style usually think poorly of themselves but see others in a good light.

An adult who feels nervous wants their partner to show approval, support, and joy. They always wish for reassurance and crave validation to calm their worries. Their partner's attention and care are like a helpful rope, a solution for their concerns and frights.

They care about their relationships but often get anxious and worry a lot about how much their partner is committed. Fear of abandonment is terrifying, and feeling safe becomes extremely important. They desire their partner's attention, care, and responsivity to calm their worried thoughts and uncertainty.

But, if support and closeness are missing or not steady, the anxious/preoccupied kind can get even more clingy, needy, and obsessed with the relationship. These people may feel an overwhelming need for love and cuddles as if their entire being relied on it. They want stability and connection, so distance or emotional unavailability makes them more anxious.

It's crucial to grasp that these worried attachment actions originate from a deeply ingrained dread of being rejected and left alone. The worried grown-up might have gone through previous situations that strengthened these worries, causing their current way of getting attached.

Here's the kicker: Research conducted by Social Psychological and Personality Science in 2017 showed that couples with either or both partners exhibit anxious-preoccupied attachment styles and are more susceptible to experiencing negative emotions like anxiety, anger, and sadness. The study tracked the experiences of 100 couples over one year and found said results. Here's a Graph showing the results (Mean scores for negative adjectives for father based on gender and attachment style):

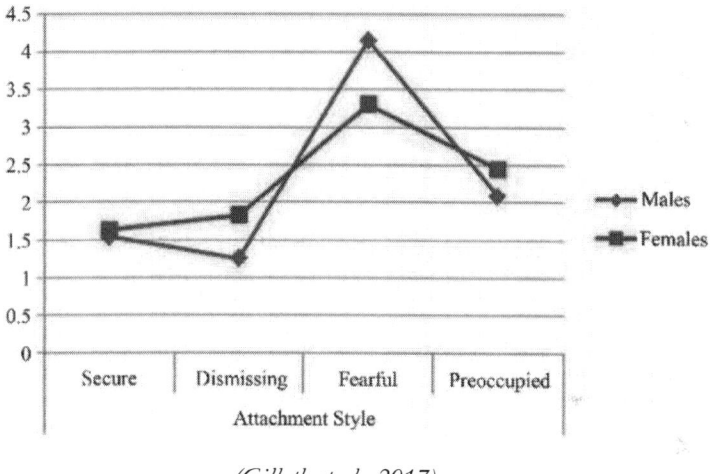

(Gillath et al., 2017)

If you connect with this attachment style, remember you're not the only one. It's essential to become aware of oneself and focus on creating a more substantial base within you. Getting therapy or support can help deal with these worries and form better ways of relating to people.

You are worthy and deserve love and care. Learning about your anxious attachment style can show you how to explore yourself and grow, leading to more inner security and stronger relationships.

- **Avoidant Attachment style - The lovers who are not emotionally available.**

    Here I should probably introduce you to Ryan and Ashley. Sure, they make a cute couple, and sure, they love each other, but when it comes to communication - all hell breaks loose - or rather - none at all. Since both are hyper-independent and don't like to rely on each other, communication isn't their strong suit. Why, you may ask? Because they're attached in an avoidant style!

    The dismissing/avoidant type typically views themselves as solitary wolves, representing power, freedom, and self-reliance. Their sense of completeness doesn't hinge on physical contact but rather on an emotional level.

    Individuals with this attachment style possess high self-esteem and hold a positive self-image. They believe deeply in what they can do and their own strong points.

    The dismissing/avoidant type does not view being in a relationship as necessary for feeling satisfied. This type doesn't want others to count on them, and they don't want to depend on others either. They don't prioritize seeking support and approval from social bonds.

    Grown-ups with this bond style usually avoid getting emotionally close. They like to keep their emotions far away, often hiding or holding them back when encountering situations that might cause strong feelings.

It's important to understand that this tendency to emotionally detach comes from wanting to shield themselves from pain or vulnerability. Their previous encounters could create a belief that depending on others or expressing their feelings may result in a letdown or being turned away.

Recognize the importance of emotional connection and vulnerability in healthy relationships if you resonate with this attachment style. Too much independence is not good, but having emotional closeness in relationships can make you feel better and happier.

Taking steps to understand yourself better and learning about why you form attachments in specific ways can help you grow and have healthier relationships. Remember, my friend, embracing and respecting your feelings is powerful, and discovering ways to handle emotional intimacy can result in stronger bonds and increased contentment in your connections.

- **Disorganized Attachment Style - The confused lovers**

    You know the cat-and-mouse chase in a relationship? Or how Katy Perry eloquently puts it in her song, "You're hot, and you're cold, you're yes then you're no" The disorganized attachment style is distinguished by unpredictable and ambiguous behaviors within interpersonal relationships. People with this attachment style frequently exhibit unpredictable relationship patterns, creating uncertainty and ambiguity for others.

    Adults with disorganized attachment styles may view their partner and the relationship as simultaneously desirable and frightening. They desire to experience intimacy and closeness, craving the accompanying emotional connection. Nevertheless, concurrently, they encounter difficulty placing trust and relying on others. Their constant internal struggle between a desire for connection and fear of vulnerability is like a never-ending battle within themselves.

Fearful-avoidant individuals long for the profound emotional connection that accompanies intimacy yet struggle with placing complete trust and dependence on others. This fear arises from previous experiences or traumatic events that have made them reluctant to embrace the potential of getting hurt. Creating a sense of distance might serve as a defense mechanism, allowing them to protect themselves by avoiding solid emotional attachments.

Individuals with a disorganized attachment style face difficulty regulating emotions is a significant challenge. The potential for them to encounter profound emotional fluctuations or grapple with efficiently managing their feelings exists. This instability may also enhance their inclination to avoid forming strong emotional bonds, as they worry about being engulfed or consumed by their emotions.

It is crucial to remember that people with a disorganized attachment style frequently bear profound wounds and fears that impact their actions and emotions. Obtaining assistance from therapy or counseling can create a secure environment to examine these hidden concerns and cultivate more adaptive methods of dealing with them.

If you resonate with this attachment style, understand that your longing for closeness and bonds is legitimate. Developing trust is imperative, both internally and within one's interpersonal connections. Opening oneself gradually and embracing vulnerability can create more profound and gratifying relationships. For university students, understanding requires effort, and it is acceptable to pursue assistance throughout the process as you explore your attachment style and develop more constructive relationship dynamics.

> **Key points:**
>
> 1. Attachment styles, such as secure, anxious-preoccupied, avoidant, and disorganized, significantly influence our relationships and how we interact with others.
>
> 2. Secure attachment provides a solid foundation of trust and love, fostering healthy relationships with safety, emotional intimacy, and independence.
>
> 3. Anxious-preoccupied attachment involves seeking reassurance and approval from partners, often accompanied by self-esteem issues and a fear of abandonment.
>
> 4. Avoidant attachment is characterized by independence, self-reliance, and difficulty forming deep emotional connections due to fear of vulnerability and dependence.
>
> 5. Disorganized attachment involves a mix of emotions and ambivalent behavior, making it challenging to regulate emotions and maintain stable relationships.

The Mind-Body Connection

"The mind and body are not separate entities; they are deeply interconnected, and together they form the foundation of our well-being."
- Deepak Chopra.

Do you recall the sensation you get when you're enthusiastic about seeing someone close to your heart? Your heart begins to race, sweat grows on your palms, and a grin stretches across your countenance. That phenomenon is called the mind-body connection, my friend!

The connection between our minds and physical bodies comes into play when we think about attachment. In fact, they work harmoniously together in influencing and shaping how we interact with others. Our experiences during childhood with caregivers wire our brains and set up the basics for our future adventures in relationships. Our brains create a guide that teaches us how to understand and cope within relationships while simultaneously generating bodily reactions accordingly.

So What Is The Mind-Body Connection?

Psychology often explores the mind-body connection, which involves closely intertwining our thoughts, emotions, and physical well-being. It acknowledges that the state of our mind and emotions can significantly affect our physical well-being and vice versa.

One way psychologists explore this connection is through a fancy term called psychoneuroimmunology. It's like a mouthful, but it looks at how stress and emotions impact our system and overall well-being. Surprisingly, how we think significantly influences the state of our physical being.

Think about it: If we're overwhelmed or feeling blue, our bodies may kick into high gear. Once stress hormones like cortisol are activated, they start affecting bodily functions and gradually weaken our resistance to various health issues. In reality, the journal Psychological Bulletin published a meta-analysis demonstrating that chronic stress has been linked to an increased probability of contracting upper respiratory infections. Our physical well-being relies heavily on the stability of our mental and emotional state, making it crucial to pay attention to both aspects.

However, positive emotions act as miniature superheroes for our bodies. When we experience joy, happiness, or gratitude, our immune system receives a boost, our hearts maintain better health, and we simply feel amazing overall. It's remarkable how our frame of indeed can genuinely influence our bodily well-being in such beneficial manners.

Our minds possess astonishing power to impact our bodies, even regarding treatments. Ever heard of placebos? They resemble enchanted sugar pills or counterfeit remedies, but can you imagine what happens next? The mere belief in their efficacy can actually result in genuine therapeutic outcomes. Our minds perceive this treatment as credible , and our bodies react accordingly. The intricate illusion our minds orchestrate upon our physical selves can be bewildering.

The placebo effect can substantially impact physical symptoms and recovery, as demonstrated by research findings.

Conversely, the nocebo effect occurs when negative expectations and beliefs about a treatment or situation result in adverse physical symptoms or outcomes.

But, of course, our minds can be sneaky too. Negative expectations and ideas can lead to what's called the nocebo effect. It's like our minds are saying, "This treatment won't work," and our bodies go, "Okay, if you say so." And suddenly, we experience adverse physical symptoms or outcomes. Our minds and bodies are definitely a quirky duo.

Exploring and embracing the intricate relationship between our minds and bodies can significantly influence our wellness. Skillful psychological strategies such as cognitive-behavioral therapy, mindfulness, and relaxation techniques can be utilized to enhance this link. They facilitate the development of optimistic thoughts, emotions, and stress management, positively impacting our mental health and contributing to physical well-being. Striking a balance between mind-body chemistry is crucial in exploiting the potential of our remarkable brains.

We must always remember that what goes on in our heads has tangible effects on our bodily state. Nurturing personal emotional stability will promote quality living with healthier and happier body conditions. It's like unlocking a distinctive superpower inherent within us all, ability we control, shaping it according to our advantage.

Body Maps of Emotions

The concept of body maps of emotions helps us comprehend the physical manifestations of our emotional states. The idea is basically that different emotions are connected to diverse physical feelings. For instance, it is common to feel sensations akin to butterflies inside our stomachs when faced with nerves or experiencing a lump in one's throat when feeling sad.

But let's get to the juicy bits. In 2013, a group of Finnish researchers induced different emotions in 701 participants and then called them to color in a body map of where they felt increasing or decreasing activity (Nummenmaa et al., 2013).

The study comprised individuals from Western European nations like Finland, Sweden, and East Asia (Taiwan).

They identified remarkable correspondences in individuals' responses without withstanding the cultural distinctions.

The body map I've created below shows some negative emotions we face and how they may affect us physically. The order of activity levels is indicated by using Black for the high and Grey for the low.

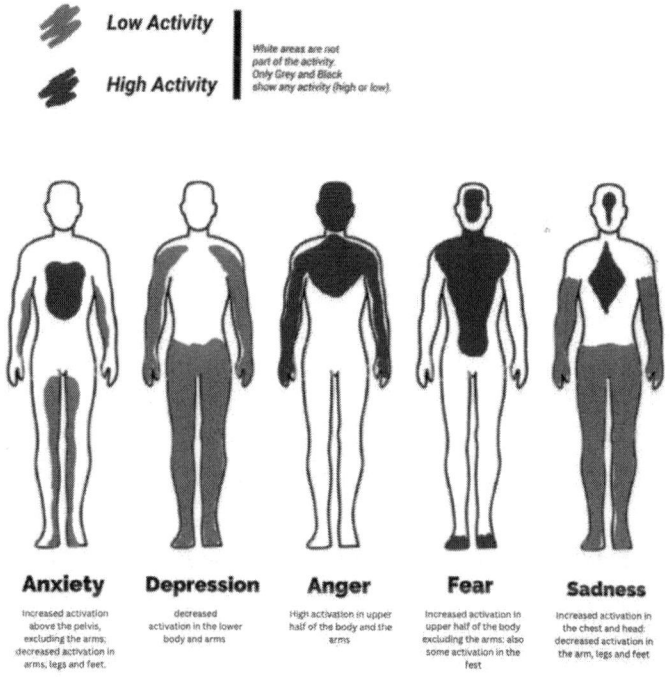

(Nummenmaa et al., 2013)

How the Mind-Body Connection Relates to Attachment

Let's look at the intriguing world of the relationship between mind and body and how it pertains to attachment styles. Picture this: you share laughter and feelings with your most intimate confidant. These moments of profound connection showcase the incredible interdependence that exists between our minds and bodies.

Attachment means establishing meaningful emotional relationships with others through feeling acknowledged, listened to, and appreciated.

Interestingly enough, our minds and bodies actively participate in this affectionate dance. A secure sense of attachment triggers an unspoken synchrony where emotions manifest into physical sensations working harmoniously like a symphony.

Don't overlook the tingly sensation that rushes over you when snuggling with someone dear or embracing another person warmly who matters deeply to you. During these blissful moments, it feels like both the body and mind commune tacitly whispering, "This is safe" or "This is love." In addition to solidifying our bonds with others, we also experience physiological responses where certain chemicals like oxytocin (the bonding hormone) course through us, leaving us feeling warm inside and anchoring us to pursue more of those magical moments. Remember Ed and Martha from earlier? They're always securely wrapped in their paranormal bundle of oxytocin.

Now let's talk about how attachments shape our well-being; bonding securely provides immense benefits for the mind and body! For instance, research indicates that having secure connections in life can result in favorable health outcomes physically by demising stress levels. Trusting relationships may reduce stress hormones such as cortisol, improving health while navigating difficult experiences. Knowing there rests a secure haven within reach alleviates anxiety-inducing situations. This ends up strengthening our bonds even more.

Furthermore, one could examine how secure attachment is a defense mechanism aiding one's immune system and leads to better health outcomes. It's a protective, rallying force against illnesses!

On the flip side, **Anxious** attachments hurt our well-being. Experiencing anxiety or disregard for our relationships may increase stress levels and debilitate our immune system. With negative thoughts moving over to physical existence, emotional turbulence thrashes around in a struggle for control. It becomes a rather aggressive game of tug of war.

Did you know that a study published in the Journal of Psychosomatic Medicine found that individuals with an insecure attachment style, specifically those with an anxious attachment style, had higher levels of inflammation markers in their bodies? Chronic inflammation is associated with various health problems, including cardiovascular disease, diabetes, and autoimmune disorders. We'll dive a bit more into that further in the chapter.

Luckily we possess the ability of self-reflection, which means that we can change our behaviors so that the connections we form strengthen our mental and physical health. Building a sturdy foundation stems from developing more productive and secure relationships leading to overall good health!

Emotions Turning Physical

Picture this: You're sitting in a crowded coffee shop, waiting for a friend who is running late. As time passes, you start feeling frustrated, worried, and impatient. And suddenly, you notice your heart pounding faster, your palms getting sweaty, and a tightness in your chest. What's going on here?

This happens because our brain communicates with various body parts through the mind-body connection. It's like a canvas where every emotion has its color and stroke.

Our feelings are more than enigmatic, abstract concepts lurking within our psyche. In fact, they considerably impact the state of our physical well-being. We share this connection between our emotions and bodies from an intricate interaction involving our brain, physiological processes, and the nervous system.

Whenever we experience emotional stimuli, complex signals travel through an extensive neural network of brains to different bodily organs leading us to undergo numerous physiological changes. These changes culminate in a broad spectrum of actual sensations. The range of physical responses one can have are *a lot*. They can range from minor cues such as butterflies or throat tightening to more impactful symptoms like sweating excessively, muscle strain, or an accelerated heart rate.

Now, let me give you the science behind it. Our autonomic nervous system (ANS) regulates functions such as breathing, heart rate, and digestion involuntarily. This system consists of two significant players: the parasympathetic nervous system (PNS) - promoting relaxation and restoration, and the sympathetic nervous system (SNS) - preparing our body for movement or action in response to intense emotions like anger or fear.

As we briefly touched upon earlier, different attachment styles can also affect how your body's unique emotional blueprint is portrayed through these physical sensations. For those with anxious attachment styles, their emotions can manifest as racing heartbeats and shallow breaths anchored by knots inside instead while feeling highly alert to protect themselves and their relationship unconsciously.

In contrast, people who are more avoidant in their attachment style might tend to disconnect from their emotions to cope with the fear of intimacy or vulnerability. They might notice a sense of numbness or tension in their body, as if they're putting up a shield to protect themselves from getting too close. It's like their body is saying, "I'm not going to let emotions overwhelm me!"

In essence, it is essential to remember that the things we feel through our attachment styles aren't just random emotions that will go away. They, instead, more often than not, fester and turn into physical symptoms that have the power to both elevate and disrupt our lives. But don't worry! Because there are several ways to change our behaviors to improve our physical health. In fact, the following section caters to this very subject.

Techniques for Cultivating Mindfulness and Body Awareness

Developing mindfulness and cultivating bodily awareness can benefit individuals dealing with attachment challenges. These techniques can potentially improve understanding of oneself, manage emotions, and foster a feeling of stability and inner connection. 'You can explore a few approaches here.'

- **Mindfulness Meditation:**

    Mindful meditation has been proven as a potent method for healing and personal development in individuals who experience challenges with attachment. Consistent mindfulness provides a secure and supportive environment to investigate attachment styles and cultivate a more profound comprehension of personal emotions and sensations.

    As reported by the study conducted by researchers and subsequently published by Psychosomatic Medicine journal in 2017, those who regularly practice mindfulness meditation experience significant reductions in their chronic pain and associated physical ailments. For 8 weeks, the study meticulously followed the journeys of 100 participants and made a noteworthy discovery - individuals who engaged in mindfulness meditation reported significantly lower pain scores. Furthermore, they exhibited a more remarkable ability to partake in activities limited by pain before.

    See it to believe it:

    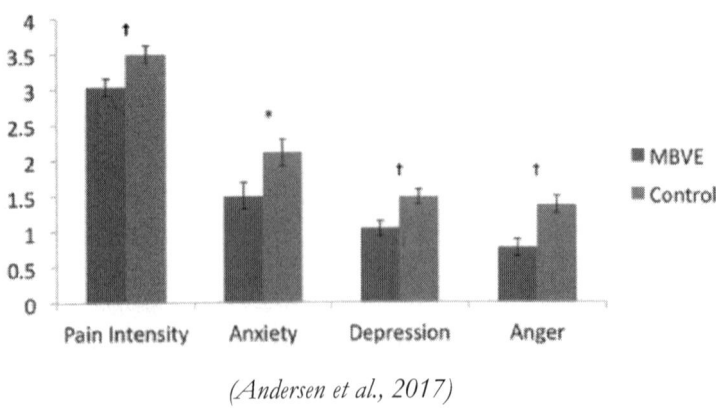

    (Andersen et al., 2017)

Mindful meditation can help us enhance our self-compassion. Specifically for those who deal with attachment issues and find it difficult to understand themselves or have low self-esteem. Mindfulness practice can be used to develop the ability to understand our thoughts and emotions without judgment, leading to self-acceptance and self-compassion.

It is recommended to seek a peaceful and inviting environment when engaging in mindfulness meditation, whether sitting upright or reclining. Begin by gradually closing your eyes or letting your gaze relax; afterward, concentrate on your breath. Focusing on the sensation of the breath entering and exiting the body helps anchor oneself in the present.

During meditation, it is normal for thoughts, emotions, and physical feelings to arise. This allows one to observe and acknowledge these experiences without becoming attached to or identifying with them. If ideas about your attachment patterns or relationships arise, watch them as passing mental events and gently redirect your attention to the breath or the present moment.

Practicing mindfulness meditation regularly allows the development of present-moment awareness. This increased level of consciousness enables you to identify the thoughts and feelings that are prompted by experiences linked to attachment. It facilitates the recognition of any patterns, reactions, or beliefs that could influence your relationships.

Mindfulness meditation assists in regulating emotions by allowing acknowledgment of solid emotions during practice, preventing impulsive reactions and overwhelming feelings.

As a result of this exercise, emotional distress in everyday life can be effectively controlled, making it easier to communicate with loved ones.

Developing mindfulness skills shaped with empathy towards yourself is necessary for improving personal growth and transformation, such as recognizing attachment needs, fears, and behaviors linked to them.

- **Body Scan**

    Including a body scan in your mindfulness practice can make all the difference when addressing attachment issues. This exercise may seem basic, but its effects are tremendous. It promotes self-acceptance and relaxation by connecting your mind with your body.

    Don't just take my word for it; actor Will Smith swears by Body scans. He said that he uses body scan meditation to help him "focus" and "clear [his] mind." He has also said that he finds it helpful for "reducing stress" and "improving [his] sleep." If the Fresh Prince of Bel-Air uses this technique, why shouldn't you?

    To start practicing it, find a comfortable spot to sit or lie in peace. Close your eyes or keep them slightly open while softening your gaze. You can take several deep breaths to calm yourself and get into the right mindset before starting.

    Start at the top of your head and slowly move downwards, paying attention to each body part. Try focusing on any sensations that arise, such as tension or emotional responses, during this exercise for optimal results.

It could be warmth, coolness, tingling, or any other exciting feeling you notice.

If you stumble upon areas of tension or discomfort, take a moment to acknowledge them without judgment. Breathe naturally and picture your breath flowing to those spots, gently releasing any tightness or stress.

You might also notice emotions bubbling up as you continue the body scan. Sometimes, emotions are physical sensations—a tight chest, a knot in your gut. That's totally normal! Let them be there without trying to push them away. Observe them with a sense of curiosity and treat yourself with kindness and compassion.

The body scan practice helps foster a deepened connection between your mind and body. By becoming more aware of the sensations and emotions experienced in each unit of your body, you can develop a heightened perception of acceptance and understanding. That is particularly good for individuals who are facing attachment concerns. The sentence offers self-awareness, allowing you to establish healthier relationships by recognizing your needs and boundaries.

The body scans helps you develop the ability to acknowledge and respect the cues your body communicates to you. This increased awareness may provide a significant understanding of your attachment patterns and how your body reacts to various relationship encounters. It enables you to become more aware of your needs and create healthier dynamics.

But wait, there's more! The process of the body scan practice extends beyond self-awareness. It's also a fantastic method for unwinding. Focusing deliberately on each body part and consciously releasing all tension allows for a profound sense of calm and liberation. It's like hitting the reset button and undoing the physiological effects of stress and anxiety that often accompany attachment issues.

As you integrate the body scan into your mindfulness practice, it is essential to maintain patience and gentleness toward yourself. Take the necessary time to thoroughly explore and pay tribute to the distinctive sensations and emotions that surface. Embrace the path of accepting and relaxing with the body scan.

- **Yoga or Tai Chi:**

    Yoga and Tai Chi provide significant advantages for individuals with attachment difficulties. Participating in such mindful movement practices can result in a substantial transformation by enhancing body awareness and fostering emotional well-being. Yoga and Tai Chi consist of gentle, continuous movements synchronizing with conscious breathing. This fusion generates a potent harmony enabling a profound connection to your physical self.

    Practicing yoga or Tai Chi allows you to achieve a mindful presence. Every movement presents itself as a chance to tune in to the sensations within your physical being. Your awareness of muscle engagement, posture alignment, and internal energy shifts increases as you practice. This increased awareness of your body helps identify and comprehend the outward signs of your emotional state and interpersonal connections.

In addition, these techniques aid in releasing physical tension stored in the body. Attachment issues frequently result in accumulating stress and anxiety, ultimately causing muscle tightness or a feeling of unease. The gentle stretches and flowing movements in yoga and Tai Chi aid in letting go of this tension, enabling energy to circulate unrestrictedly within your body. You also make room for emotional and energetic release by releasing physical tension.

A study published by Suodi Xu, Julien S. Baker, and Feng Ren in 2021 to MDPI explored the positive role of Tai Chi in responding to the stress caused by the COVID-19 Pandemic.

Engaging in these various practices, you develop a profound connection bridging your physical self and mental state. You learn to fully embrace the present moment and inhabit your physical form. This grounding and embodiment are essential for individuals who struggle with attachment issues because it assists in mitigating feelings of disconnection and promotes an enduring sense of stability and inner security.

Furthermore, engaging in yoga or Tai Chi allows individuals to regulate emotions. The amalgamation of motion, respiration, and mindfulness establishes a secure and supportive environment to delve into your feelings. As you progress in practice, you might encounter various emotions that emerge and fade away. By observing these emotions without judgment and allowing them to flow, you cultivate emotional resilience and regulation skills. The newfound capability to navigate and regulate emotions can significantly influence one's attachment style and relationship approach.

Engaging in yoga or Tai Chi provides a comprehensive method of addressing attachment issues through holistic healing. These mindful movement practices help you develop a sense of embodiment, cultivate body awareness, release tension, and regulate your emotions. By engaging in regular and dedicated practice, you can enhance your connection with yourself, nurture emotional well-being, and cultivate healthier dynamics within relationships. So, lay out your yoga mat or locate a peaceful area for Tai Chi, and begin an enlightening expedition of exploring oneself and finding solace.

- **Somatic Experiencing:**

    Somatic Experiencing is a highly valuable methodology for people with attachment-related challenges. This modality addresses and resolves stored trauma or stress within the body. The process acknowledges that traumatic occurrences can stay confined within our bodies, influencing emotional welfare and attachment patterns. Through active participation in Somatic Experiencing, You can commence a transformative process of healing and rejuvenation.

    In Somatic Experiencing sessions, individuals are gently guided by a skilled therapist to explore bodily sensations, movements, and gestures. This process helps individuals create a secure and encouraging setting to reconnect with their bodies and release stored tension or trauma. The therapist supports individuals in accessing the delicate sensations within their bodies, thus enabling a more profound comprehension of the physical expressions related to their attachment concerns.

This therapeutic approach encourages individuals to observe and investigate their physical sensations without forming opinions or anticipations. Through nurturing a caring and unbiased mindset towards their own experiences, people can initiate the process of untangling and letting go of any distressing imprints that could have affected their way of forming connections. This procedure facilitates the recovery of a feeling of security within the physical being, enabling people to develop more beneficial connection habits.

Collaborating with a skilled therapist in Somatic Experiencing is essential for navigating this healing journey. By establishing a secure atmosphere, these therapists willingly assist patients along their path to recovery by providing steadfast guidance and support at each stage.

Someone I knew, let's call her Kelsey, had a history of abandonment issues. Her father was an alcoholic, and her mother left her when she was only 11. Kelsey found that somatic experiencing helped her connect with her emotions and physical sensations. She was able to start to understand how her body held onto the pain of her past experiences, and she was able to begin to release it.

Like Kelsey, Somatic Experiencing allows individuals to tackle and overcome the deep-rooted traumas that might have influenced their attachment patterns. By physically removing and integrating these experiences, people can cultivate a stronger feeling of security, reliance, and adaptability within themselves and in their interactions. This therapeutic approach can potentially change attachment patterns and create opportunities for more rewarding and secure relationships with others.

Acknowledging the importance of experienced professionals in Somatic Experiencing is crucial. Their specialization allows them to support individuals with unique attachment disorders, ultimately aiding their healing journey. Through the collaborative efforts of the therapist and the individual, Somatic Experiencing can become a powerful tool for unraveling the complexities of attachment and fostering profound transformation and growth.

- **Journaling:**

    Journaling is a surprisingly effective approach that anyone can use to gain insight into attachment issues. By setting aside small portions of time to analyze your feelings, ideas, and bodily sensations each day, you initiate a space for self-discovery and introspection. Simply grab a pen and paper, seek out a tranquil area so that the ideas readily come, then express yourself through writing!

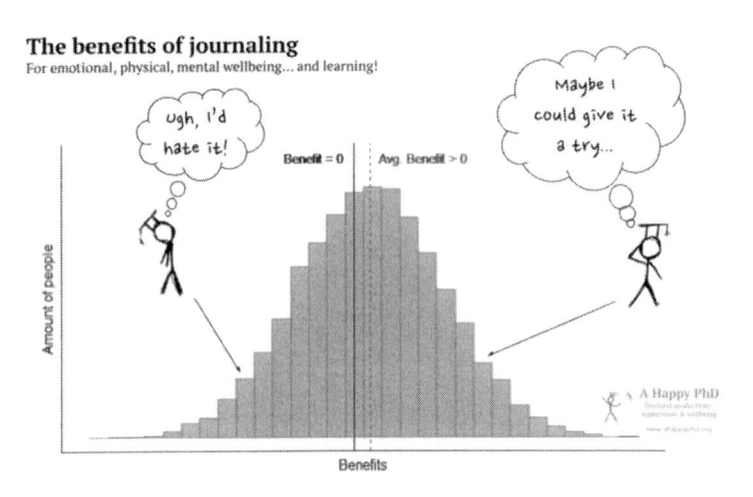

The benefits of journaling
For emotional, physical, mental wellbeing... and learning!

(Luis P. Prieto, 2021)

The findings shown in the graph above demonstrate a correlation between the act of journaling and the reduction of anxiety. The study observed that those who dedicated 20 minutes of their day to journaling consistently for 8 weeks encountered significant alleviation in anxiety symptoms, contrasting the outcomes seen among individuals in the control group.

When journaling about attachment issues, begin by exploring your experiences and relationships. Notice any patterns or recurring themes that emerge. Are there specific triggers that elicit strong emotional responses or physical sensations? Write about these moments, capturing the nuances and complexities of your attachment dynamics. Give yourself the freedom to express your emotions without limitation or criticism to convey the pleasures and difficulties accompanying emotional bonds.

As you explore your journaling habit further, keep track of how your thoughts, feelings, and physical sensations are connected. Notice how certain thoughts or memories may trigger specific bodily reactions. Perhaps you feel a tightening in your chest when you recall a past relationship or a surge of anxiety when contemplating vulnerability. Describe your experiences concerning the link between mind and body and analyze how your attachment style materializes in your physical being.

Don't underestimate the power of journaling to grant a space for contemplating and examining yourself. Utilize this chance to scrutinize your opinions about relationships, attachments, and self-concept. Are there any self-limiting beliefs or negative self-perceptions that influence your attachment patterns? Write about these beliefs and challenge them with compassionate and realistic counter-narratives. Showing a light on your internal landscape can give you a deeper understanding of yourself and your attachment style.

Apart from reflection and self-expression, journaling can also provide clarity and guidance. Utilize your journal as a medium to establish intentions, objectives, and confirmations regarding your attachment venture. Describe the connections you seek and the characteristics you aim to develop within yourself. The relationships you aspire to create should be envisioned as secure and fulfilling. Writing down your desires and aspirations allows you to clarify them and attract their manifestation in your life.

Journaling, rest assured, is an individual and confidential habit. There are no guidelines or requirements for expressing oneself through writing. Permit your thoughts to move without restraint, allowing yourself to show vulnerability and authenticity. Discover yourself and grow through the process of journaling. As you review your entries over time, you might observe patterns, advancements, and newfound wisdom that can help steer you toward fostering healthier attachments on your path.

Thus, take hold of that notebook and allow your pen to gracefully glide over the sheets. Discover your attachment experiences, unravel the complexities of your thoughts and emotions, and cultivate a stronger bond with yourself. Journaling is a beneficial tool that aids in comprehending, revitalizing, and nurturing stable and rewarding connections.

Key points:

1. The mind-body connection refers to the influence of thoughts, emotions, and sensations on physical health and well-being.

2. Emotions and sensations manifest in the body, and our attachment styles can affect how we experience and express them.

3. Techniques like mindful meditation, body scan, yoga or Tai Chi, and somatic experiencing can cultivate body awareness, promote emotional well-being, and aid in healing attachment issues.

4. Journaling is a valuable tool for self-reflection and exploring attachment-related thoughts, emotions, and patterns.

5. Working on attachment-related issues and healing is never too late. With self-reflection, self-compassion, and a willingness to grow, individuals can make significant progress in creating healthier attachment patterns and experiencing more fulfilling relationships.

Healing Attachment Wounds

"The journey of healing attachment wounds is not easy, but it is worth it. By acknowledging our past, embracing our vulnerability, and learning to love ourselves, we can rewrite our story and create the secure and fulfilling connections we deserve." - Brené Brown

Brown describes the process of recognizing and understanding wounds connected to attachment as a brave and transformative journey that numerous individuals engage in while seeking healing and personal growth. These wounds can run deep, shaping our beliefs, behaviors, and relationship patterns. Still, by shedding a compassionate light on these wounds, we can begin comprehending their complexities, establishing a foundation for healing, and fostering healthier attachments.

Recognizing and Understanding Attachment-Related Wounds

First, it is vital to learn that attachment-related wounds can have diverse sources like childhood experiences, past traumas, or significant losses. Manifestations of these wounds could be seen as a fear of intimacy, trouble placing trust in others, or a constant need for validation and assurance. They can leave us feeling vulnerable, guarded, or disconnected from our emotions.

Understanding these wounds requires us to explore our backgrounds and carefully examine the consistent patterns manifested in our interactions. Allocate some time for self-reflection on significant milestones in your life, instances of rejection or being left alone, and any emotions that still need resolution that could have influenced how you relate to others. Accepting and confirming these experiences allows us to cultivate greater self-awareness and empathy.

It is crucial to tackle this process with kindness and gentleness for ourselves. Comprehend that these wounds are not faults or limitations but human responses to challenging conditions. Grant yourself permission to embrace the surface emotions, be it sadness, anger, or confusion. Always remember that healing isn't a linear journey, and moving forward gradually is okay.

Once you understand your attachment-related wounds more deeply, you might start recognizing their influence on your present relationships and interactions. Be vigilant in noticing recurring patterns, triggers, and emotional reactions that emerge during your interactions with others. I wonder how these wounds influence your expectations, fears, and desires in relationships. When you illuminate these patterns, you allow yourself to make mindful decisions and escape from detrimental cycles.

Seeking help from trustworthy friends, family, or experts can be highly advantageous on this voyage of acknowledgment and comprehension. Share your experiences and struggles with someone who can offer empathy and guidance. Therapy or counseling provides a secure environment to examine your attachment wounds and make progress toward healing. Always remember, there's support available if you don't want to travel alone on this path.

While on the journey of healing, be patient with yourself. To experience healing, one must invest time and effort; however, the gains are beyond measure. Uncovering the different layers of these wounds opens up opportunities for personal growth, kindness towards oneself, and the fostering of healthier connections. You hold the potential to redefine your story, welcome vulnerability, and nurture authentic and impactful relationships with others.

So what are you waiting for? embrace this expedition of acknowledgment and understanding with a receptive heart. Welcome the scars as guides and stimulants for advancement. By honoring your experiences and tending to your attachment wounds, you embark on a transformative path toward greater self-awareness, healing, and the potential for nurturing and fulfilling relationships.

Importance of Self-Compassion And Self-Care In Healing

When in the process of healing, it is crucial to be mindful of our humanity. As flawed human beings, we all experience moments of difficulty. This is where self-compassion becomes a necessary part of our healing journey.

Self-compassion involves treating ourselves with kindness and acceptance. Just like how we would treat a dear friend going through tough times. We must accept and validate our emotions while offering ourselves love and support.

Healing attachment wounds can be pretty challenging, requiring time and patience. Judging ourselves harshly or feeling disheartened if progress seems slow is easy. However, setbacks are an intrinsic element in this non-linear healing path.

This is where practicing self-kindness slides in. By understanding that we cannot change the past, we become more gentle with ourselves and forgive ourselves for any shortcomings.

Taking care of oneself physically, emotionally, and intellectually comes under the umbrella term Self-Care. Self-care plays an essential part in the pathway to recovery as it serves the function of not being selfish but instead giving necessary attention to ourselves. Self-care is basically anything that brings you joy.

There are many fundamental aspects to remember when engaging with self-care techniques, from enjoying soaking up life's pleasures in nature to practicing mindfulness regularly. From upholding healthy habits by eating correctly to enjoying tasty treats every once in a while.

Practicing self-compassion and self-care creates a supportive foundation for our healing process. In moments of struggle, we realize how crucial it is to be there for ourselves, respect our emotions, and prioritize self-care. By undertaking these acts of self-kindness and self-nurturing, we open up the possibility for healing and transformation.

Remind yourself that you should be shown compassion and care. Embrace your path with affection and gentleness, and acknowledge that healing can occur. By implementing the suggestions and secrets I am about to disclose, trust me when I say that success will come your way quickly!

Exercises and Techniques for Healing Past Attachment Wounds

How about we now look at some activities and techniques for healing past attachment wounds fun and healthily? Remember that healing is a personal voyage, so don't be afraid to customize these techniques according to your wants and preferences.

- **Inner-Child work**

    Inner Child Work, a powerful practice for healing, aids in reuniting individuals with their injured inner selves that have been influenced by previous attachment experiences. By picturing yourself as a child, you can access the emotions and wants that may have been ignored or underserved at that moment. You can use this occasion to offer love, support, and validation to that vulnerable aspect of yourself.

    To participate in inner child work, locate a calm and cozy area where you can contemplate and visualize yourself as a young child. Visualize how you were during different stages of your younger years. Consider for a moment your state of mind and emotions during those impactful times in the past. Consider any feelings like gloominess, apprehension, wrathfulness, or even contentment.

    As you establish a link with your younger self, it is vital to extend unconditional love and aid to them - the kind they probably desired all along. Envision embracing them with understanding and solace. Conveying messages of comfort and motivation plays a vital role in emphasizing the value of pursuing love, security, and happiness.

Regarding inner child work, it is crucial to allocate some time for engaging in fun little activities that awaken playfulness within us. Rekindle your childhood passions by making time for hobbies like drawing, dancing, playing musical instruments, or spending time outdoors. In such a way, you can genuinely understand the joyful liberty that accompanies sparking your inner child. For example, a friend of mine used to love playing with dolls as a young girl, and it had always brought her comfort; as she grew older, she began molding and painting clay dolls and selling them. Not only did this help with her anxiety, but it even left her with a fun side hustle!

Caring for your inner child has profound healing powers that can help change your perspective on life. You can recognize and deal with the hurts that might have influenced your way of forming connections and affected your relationships. By giving love, support, and validation to your inner child that may have been missing, you can start healing those attachment wounds and forming a healthier bond with yourself and others.

Remember, inner child work is a gradual and ongoing process. Give yourself patience and understanding as you travel on this path of healing. It's typical to come across resistance or challenging emotions as you go. If tackling this task independently feels overwhelming, you may seek guidance from a proficient expert in inner child healing, such as a therapist or counselor.

By looking after your younger self, you can set a solid base for healing emotional hurts and fostering deep relationships.

Approach this practice by being nice, soft, and ready to reconnect with the valuable parts of yourself that need healing and love.

- **Guided visualization**

    Guided visualization is a fantastic tool that taps into the imagination and allows you to create a safe and nurturing space within your mind. It offers a way to access healing and transformative experiences by engaging your senses and emotions.

    First, find a tranquil and cozy spot soothing enough for relaxation without disturbances. Take some deep breaths and slip into a state of calmness and relaxation while shutting your eyes. Once serene in this peaceful state, envisage yourself in a calming environment where you feel secure, at ease, and cared for. The spot could be an idyllic beach, a serene forest teeming with life, or perhaps even a meditative garden; any place that adds comfort to your soul will suffice.

    Once you've chosen your safe space, populate it with loving and supportive figures. Trusted friends, family, or even imagined spiritual or wise beings are options. Imagine being surrounded by their presence and feeling their warm love wrap around you. Picture yourself surrounded by their support, encouragement, and acceptance in this visualization.

    Let your emotions flow and experience them completely in this imagined situation. Feel the security, comfort, and acceptance from the figures surrounding you. Feel these sensations deeply within you, comforting any emotional hurts and revitalizing your essence.

During the guided visualization, you can also engage your senses. Notice the sights, sounds, and scents of your chosen environment. Embrace the cozy vibes of sunshine, a delicate breeze, or a soft rug beneath you. Engross yourself in every intricate detail, amplifying the liveliness of the experience tenfold!

When you are in this healing space, you can decide to have conversations with the supportive figures around you. Let them know your emotions, fears, and needs. Allow their loving responses to bring you comfort and assurance. Spend as long as you want to picture yourself in this comforting bubble, allowing it to cleanse any lingering discomfort or uncertainties.

A young woman who had gone through the tremendous trauma of losing her husband used guided visualization to heal her emotional wounds. Imagining herself in the past, she would see herself when her partner passed, but she would view herself from the perspective of her grandmother, who had always loved and cared for her. She would visualize Gran giving her the affection and assistance she desired back then. Gradually, she discovered that she had the power to alleviate herself from the accumulated pain and hurt. She found solace in this imagery, allowing her to progress and shape a more optimistic future.

What's even better about guided visualizations is that it is an activity that can be personalized to suit your particular wants and needs. You can explore different variations and adapt them to fit your healing journey. Some individuals value listening to recorded guided visualization sessions, whereas others create personal visualizations inspired by their distinct experiences and aspirations.

Just remember that guided visualization is a technique for exploring yourself and finding healing, but it could take some time to see significant changes. Keep practicing regularly and try to go deeper into the experience each time. Be gentle and patient with yourself, as healing attachment wounds is gradual.

By participating in guided visualizations, we can find emotional healing, care for ourselves, and feel safer and more supported. This practice is beneficial for reshaping unhealthy attachment patterns, promoting greater self-compassion, and enhancing relationships with others.

Guided visualization can be utilized independently or with the guidance of a therapist or meditation instructor. No matter what route you choose, this tool is effective in healing attachment wounds and promoting personal development. Welcome the visualization process with a kind and curious attitude as you discover the power of healing within yourself.

- **Emotional Freedom Techniques (EFT) tapping**

    EFT tapping is a compelling and easily accessible method for healing attachment wounds. This technique incorporates traditional Chinese medicine and modern psychology to unlock emotional barriers and foster profound healing. EFT tapping involves gently tapping specific meridian points on the body while verbalizing your feelings and emotions.

    And guess what? Science totally backs up this technique. An article published in the Journal of Couple and Family

Psychology in 2016 highlighted how EFT effectively decreased attachment anxiety and avoidance within couples. The research observed 60 couples who were randomly divided into two groups: EFT and a control group. The results obtained after 12 weeks of therapeutic intervention revealed that couples engaged in the EFT group witnessed significant reductions in both attachment anxiety and avoidance, accompanied by notable enhancements in their overall relationship satisfaction.

So how do you begin EFT tapping? start by finding a peaceful and pleasant space where you can channel your focus toward exploring your emotions with minimal disruption. Pause and listen to your body to discover the emotions or memories connected to your attachment wounds. Be aware of any strain, unease, or weightiness that could be there.

You can begin the EFT tapping procedure after identifying the emotions or memories. Tap lightly with your fingertips on the particular meridian points on your body. Note that you should target specific spots above your forehead near the hairline or eyebrows, including sides next to the eyes and lower portions beneath the eyes or around the nose. Plus, don't overlook areas like the chin or neckline while reaching out underneath the arms. Incorporate the practice of acknowledging and validating youremotions by repeating an affirmation while tapping.

If you are experiencing feelings of abandonment or fear from attachment wounds, you can try saying, 'Despite feeling abandoned and scared, I genuinely love and accept myself.' Repeat this affirmation or a similar one while tapping on each meridian point. Tapping while vocalizing your emotions is a powerful technique to eliminate emotional blockages and bring equilibrium to your energy system.

As you proceed with tapping, you might detect alterations in your feelings, sensations, or thoughts. Allowing whatever exists without judgment or resistance is of utmost significance. If new memories or feelings arise, acknowledge them and incorporate them into your tapping practice.

Make EFT tapping personal by modifying it to suit your individual needs. Feel free to alter the locations you tap on, experiment with various affirmations, or explore different intensities and tempos during your tapping practice. Believe in your gut feelings and follow them to discover the right approach.

EFT tapping requires a consistent commitment for optimal outcomes. Consistent practice enables more profound healing and integration of your tasks. Incorporating EFT tapping into your everyday self-care routine allows you to allocate specific time to heal your attachment wounds and actively engage in the tapping technique. As time passes, you might observe a decrease in the strength of your emotions, enhanced self-compassion, and an improved sense of emotional well-being.

Although EFT tapping can be carried out alone, collaborating with a certified EFT practitioner can offer extra assistance and guidance. They can support you in maneuvering through complex emotions and offer valuable perspectives on your attachment patterns. A practitioner can also provide personalized tapping sequences and facilitate a safe space for healing.

Healing attachment wounds is a journey that demands time and patience. Allowing yourself to embrace self-compassion and gentleness when practicing EFT tapping can amplify its effectiveness on your journey. Allow yourself to be receptive to the emotions and memories that surface while tapping, and respect your healing journey at your own rhythm.

Including EFT tapping in your healing practice enables you to release emotional blockages, promote self-compassion, and form a pathway for healing attachment wounds. Embrace this method's strength as you embark on your expedition towards increased emotional well-being and more fulfilling relationships.

- **Affirmations**

    Utilizing affirmations as a strategy can assist in reshaping your mindset and nurturing feelings of self-compassion and self-worth as you navigate healing from attachment wounds. They address negative beliefs and thoughts that may have originated from past experiences. By repeating positive and empowering statements, you can gradually shift your perspective and create new neural pathways that support your healing journey.

    You should know that a 2017 study in the Journal of Positive Psychology suggests positive affirmations can enhance cognitive abilities. The study consisted of 60 randomly allocated participants into two groups: one that engaged in positive affirmations and another that formed the control group. A considerable boost was seen in memory and problem-solving proficiency and enhanced self-esteem among participants assigned to the affirmation group for 12 weeks.

Don't believe me? See it to believe it!

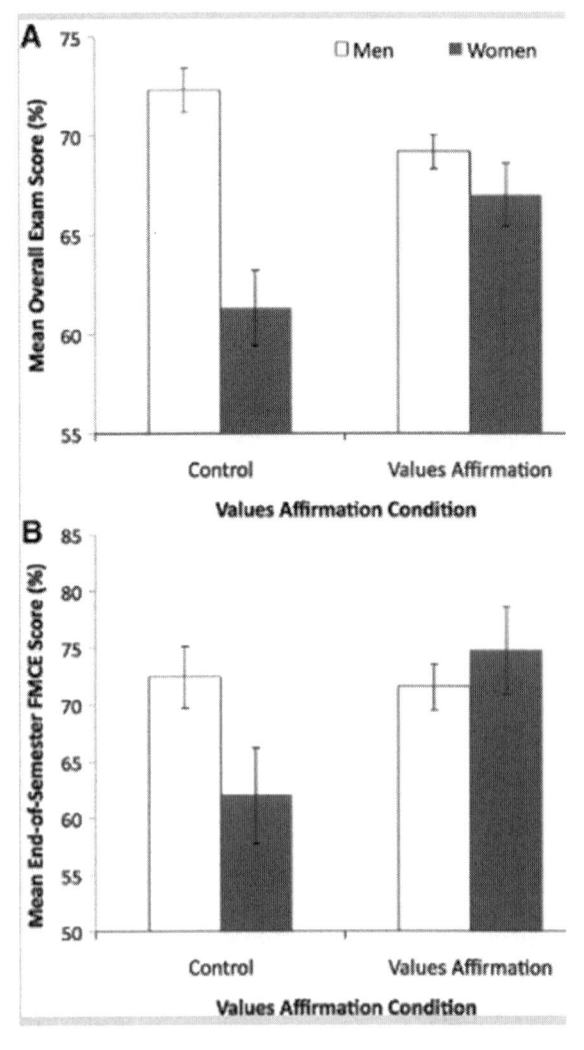

(Creswell et al., 2017)

While constructing affirmations, choosing words and phrases that hold a personal solid resonance is essential. Consider the specific attachment wounds you are addressing and the qualities and beliefs you aim to foster. Here are some examples of affirmations that can support your healing process:

- "I am deserving of love and healthy relationships." This affirmation reminds you that you are worthy of love and can form healthy and fulfilling connections with others.

- "I am lovable and worthy of belonging." This affirmation counters feelings of unworthiness or isolation that may have stemmed from past attachment wounds. It affirms your inherent value and the importance of connection.

- "I release fear and embrace vulnerability in relationships." This affirmation helps you overcome fear and resistance and invites a sense of openness and vulnerability, which is essential for building secure and meaningful connections.

- "I am enough exactly as I am." This affirmation emphasizes self-acceptance and self-worth, reminding you that you don't need to strive for perfection or seek external validation to be deserving of love and belonging.

- "I trust myself to make healthy relationship choices." This affirmation empowers you to trust your instincts and make decisions that align with your emotional well-being. It encourages self-reliance and self-trust.

- "I forgive myself and others for past hurts." This affirmation acknowledges the pain and hurt that may have been caused by attachment wounds and invites forgiveness for yourself and others involved. It allows you to release emotional burdens and create space for healing.

- "I am capable of creating secure and loving connections." This affirmation instills confidence in your ability to form secure and loving relationships. It affirms that you can break free from negative attachment patterns and create healthy dynamics.

Maintain a routine of regularly saying these affirmations, ideally every day. Adding them to your morning or evening routine or whenever you feel like being gently reminded about how far you've come on your healing journey is worth considering. Declare them with belief and focus, allowing the affirming words to resonate within your subconsciousness.

Besides using verbal affirmations, you can also record them in a journal or make visual reminders like sticky notes or affirmation cards to display in prominent areas. These positive affirmations around you can constantly remind you of your worthiness and the continuous progress in your healing.

In the process of using affirmations, treat yourself with gentleness and patience. The healing of attachment wounds takes time, and it is expected to have occasional doubts or resistance. Have faith in the journey and embrace positive affirmations that deeply connect with your heart and encourage personal development.

Consistent affirmation practice can rewire your mindset, bolster your self-compassion, and nurture a profound belief in yourself. Over time, these positive beliefs will mold your experiences and interactions, allowing you to heal from attachment wounds and create a nourishing and enriching existence.

To conclude, the techniques discussed for healing attachment wounds furnish valuable instruments and exercises to support your progress toward emotional healing and self-development. Each method brings its own exclusive benefits and approaches; however, they all center around cultivating self-compassion, self-awareness, and self-care.

Key Points:

1. Healing attachment wounds is a process that requires patience, self-compassion, and dedication.

2. Inner child work allows you to connect with and nurture the vulnerable parts of yourself that may have experienced attachment wounds.

3. Guided visualizations create a safe and nurturing space within your imagination, helping you experience feelings of security and acceptance.

4. EFT tapping offers a physical and emotional release by tapping on specific meridian points while acknowledging and verbalizing your emotions.

5. Affirmations are potent tools for rewiring your mindset and cultivating self-compassion and self-worth.

6. Consistency is vital in incorporating these techniques into your daily self-care routine.

7. Tailoring the techniques to your individual needs and preferences is essential.

8. Seeking support from qualified professionals can provide guidance and assistance on your healing journey.

9. Embrace the power of self-compassion, self-awareness, and self-care as you embark on the transformative healing of attachment wounds.

10. Gradually healing attachment wounds can lead to healthier attachment styles and more fulfilling connections.

Developing Authentic Connections

"Authenticity is a collection of choices we must make daily. It's about the choice to show up and be real. The choice, to be honest. The choice to let our true selves be seen." - Brené Brown

Genuine connections are like magic, but sometimes it feels like obstacles are everywhere, right? With social media pushing us to showcase only our highlight reel and society telling us to fit into molds, authenticity can be a real challenge. But fear not! Join me as we examine these barriers, deconstruct them, and unveil tactics to break free. By embracing this perspective, we unleash a universe of natural and enjoyable interactions with fantastic individuals. Let's be realistic and ensure those connections have value!

We can't deny the existence of social norms that can hinder our self-confidence as we constantly worry about gaining other people's approval. Every person has concerns that trouble them. But guess what? We're up for the challenge! Understanding why barriers exist and how much they affect us can help us overcome them. We strive to form friendships and enjoy exciting experiences that bring genuine happiness.

So, get ready! In this section, we're exploring the fantastic realm of authenticity. Count on us for valuable insights and practical tips to master creating genuine connections like a professional. Ready yourself for flourishing and thriving in your relationships.

Exploration of Authentic Connections in Relationships:

- **Building Trust: The Foundation of Authenticity**

  Genuine connections rely on trust as their underlying basis. It serves as the unseen connection that runs through relationships, nurturing a feeling of comfort, assurance, and transparency. To truly understand how trust influences the development of authentic connections, we need to analyze its link with attachment styles and appreciate the meaning of vulnerability.

  Establishing trust is vital in creating genuine bonds, generating a feeling of dependability and consistency. Fostering a sense of comfort and security creates a firm ground for individuals to be themselves. When there is trust, people can openly share their thoughts, emotions, and weaknesses without judgment or feeling betrayed.

  The lasting impact of our experiences with caregivers during childhood can significantly shape our adult perspective on trust. It's akin to figuring out a complex puzzle, you know? Those with secure attachment styles have this awesome foundation of trust. They have discovered that their requirements will be consistently fulfilled, and they can depend on others without any concerns. They've got confidence in the reliability of their peeps and are totally cool with leaning on them for support.

  There's even more to it - Anxious or avoidant attachment styles can throw some hurdles our way. Anxiously attached folks might struggle with trust due to those nagging fears of being left behind or rejected. It's like their trust-o-meter has some glitches. On the other hand, avoidantly attached individuals are a bit guarded. Their fear of dependency and vulnerability makes trusting others a challenge for them.

It's like a rollercoaster ride. Don't worry; the key to successfully navigating the twists and turns lies in comprehending these attachment styles and their influence on trust. Secure yourself in for an exciting ride as we unveil strategies to nurture trust and form extraordinary connections that last a lifetime!

Imagine vulnerability as the special ingredient that propels trust and fosters deeper connections. The essence lies in having the bravery to uncover our true selves completely - the desirable qualities and the flaws - before a special person. When we embrace vulnerability, we send a powerful message: "Hey, I trust you with the real me!"

And here's the magical part: those genuine and heartfelt moments where individuals show their vulnerability? They're like superglue for authentic connections. Creating an open dialogue about our fears, insecurities, and emotions helps cultivate a safe space for trust to grow. My friend, the interaction goes both ways. When both participants feel sufficiently safe to expose their vulnerabilities, they commence an awe-inspiring voyage hand in hand. They truly get each other, building empathy and forging an unbreakable bond.

Let's fully embrace our vulnerability! This undisclosed component enables us to establish sincere connections and draws us towards individuals who genuinely empathize with and hold dear our unique selves.

Trust doesn't develop overnight; it necessitates consistent time and effort. Actions that consistently display reliability, honesty, and empathy are required. Opening up to vulnerability and being open to others' vulnerabilities can create deeper and more authentic bonds.

- **Emotional Intimacy: The Power of Authentic Sharing**

    Emotional intimacy is important in genuine connections. It extends beyond the shallow and explores the intricacies of our emotional landscapes, fostering a meaningful connection among individuals. Now let's delve into the significance of emotional closeness, its intricate link to attachment patterns, and effective techniques for establishing a secure environment that encourages transparent and sincere communication.

    Like the secret sauce enhances a dish, emotional intimacy enhances relationships and takes them to extraordinary heights! It feels like an enchanting waltz of connection, faith, and empathy that joins two hearts. Through the experience of emotional closeness, a holy space is formed where we have the freedom to expose our vulnerable selves and feel secure in receiving compassion and affirmation.

    Here's the thing: Profound connections can be achieved through emotional intimacy. It revolves around being receptive and transparent in revealing our innermost musings, sentiments, and unique encounters. The key is to embrace vulnerability, understanding that our partner will genuinely see and treasure us for the individuals we are.

But guess what? Additionally, our attachment styles factor in here! Thanks to the reliable care and support they have received, those with secure attachments are naturally inclined towards emotional intimacy. They feel at ease expressing their emotions and receiving those of their partner. Their emotional prowess is akin to having superpowers! We create an everlasting bond overflowing with love when we nurture a sense of closeness, trustworthiness, and comprehension.

Nonetheless, attachment styles can also generate struggles. Anxiously attached individuals may yearn for emotional closeness yet simultaneously fear rejection or abandonment. This could cause a struggle in openly expressing emotions or constantly seeking reassurance. Those with an avoidantly attached style may struggle with engaging in intimate emotions, often choosing to suppress feelings or maintain emotional boundaries for self-preservation.

Several strategies can be employed to foster a safe space that encourages open and honest communication:

Get Your Active Listening On: Demonstrate to your partner that they have your complete focus. Listen with empathy, really understanding their perspective. Acknowledge their emotions and assure them of your support. Ensure that the dialogue remains open without any criticism or judgment.

Tune in to Emotional Awareness: Promote being introspective about your emotions and encourage open discussions with your partner. Formulate an environment that promotes the unrestricted expression and exploration of emotions, eliminating anxiety regarding criticism or mockery.

It's all about nurturing a climate of emotional accessibility and empathy.

Trust-Building Adventures: Engage in trust-building activities that encourage vulnerability and deep connection. Exchange personal narratives, participate in activities that enhance trustworthiness, and stand united during vulnerability. These activities create a solid framework for promoting safety and honesty.

Embrace Honesty and Authenticity: Just be real! Foster open and honest communication by being your most honest self. Foster a supportive environment that enables both partners to confidently voice their genuine thoughts and emotions, free from the fear of judgment. Being genuine and supporting your partner's authenticity is what matters.

Developing emotional closeness necessitates patience, commitment, and joint dedication in a romantic partnership. Building trust, vulnerability, and open communication require dedication.

Understanding and Overcoming Barriers to Authenticity:

- **Fear of Rejection: Embracing Vulnerability**

    The feeling of fear when facing potential rejection often comes from our strong desire for acceptance and belonging. The thought of not being accepted or valued by others arises when contemplating the possibility of revealing our true selves. So, what do we do? We don masks, feigning to be someone we aren't. But here's the kicker: Our apprehension hinders us from embracing our authenticity and building the authentic connections we crave.

Don't sweat it, though. We can triumph over this fear and release our genuine identities. It all starts by cultivating acceptance of ourselves and summoning the bravery to accept and celebrate who we are. Join us as we uncover practical techniques to empower us to overcome fear and embody our authentic greatness. The fear we experience limits our authenticity and obstructs genuine connections from forming.

Attachment anxiety, influenced by our attachment styles, can intensify the fear of rejection. People who exhibit anxious attachment styles frequently face intensified worries regarding their deservingness of love and acceptance. They may constantly seek reassurance and validation from others, fearing abandonment or disapproval. The anxiety attached to this fear intensifies the fear of being rejected for their authentic selves.

To overcome the fear of rejection and embrace vulnerability:

Cultivate Self-Acceptance: Show yourself some love! Develop self-acceptance and compassion. Remember, your worthiness isn't dependent on others' opinions. Embrace your capabilities and acknowledge that flaws are a common element of the human condition.

Challenge Negative Beliefs: Say goodbye to those self-defeating thoughts as we expose their flaws! Investigate the harmful beliefs that sustain the fear of rejection. Ask yourself if they hold true or if alternative perspectives are possible. Transform your mindset by replacing negativity with empowering thoughts.

Practice Gradual Exposure: Progress gradually by tackling smaller steps. Commence by opening up to trusted individuals who have proved their acceptance and support in the past, sharing your thoughts and feelings with them. As you gain assurance, incrementally stretch the limits of what feels familiar to you, letting your genuine self shine through.

Seek Support: Teamwork makes the dream work! Establish supportive bonds with others or pursue therapy to confront and understand the underlying factors contributing to your fear of rejection. A therapist can guide you and provide coping strategies to overcome this fear.

Embrace Resilience: Remember that rejection is an inevitable part of life, but it should never define your inherent value. Embrace your resilience! See rejections as chances to develop personally and explore oneself. They can be stepping stones to greater things.

Embracing vulnerability demands both courage and self-compassion. This transformative journey lets you let go of fear and confidently embody your authentic self. By nurturing self-acceptance and facing the fear of rejection head-on, you open doors to genuine connections and meaningful relationships.

- **Social Expectations and Masks: Unveiling Your True Self**

  When striving for genuine connections, one must acknowledge how social expectations and the false personas we often adopt can shape our behavior by societal norms.

Understand how societal standards and expectations shape our behavior. The impact of outside forces can lead us down a path where we feel compelled to conceal our true selves and portray an artificial image that conforms. But guess what? Our mission is to recapture our genuine selves and promote authentic connections.

The way we attach to others also influences our conformity to societal norms. Anxiously attached people may seek external validation and conform easily to avoid rejection. **Avoidantly** attached folks may use masks to maintain emotional distance and protect themselves. Nevertheless, we are escaping from these patterns!

To escape the confines of societal pressures and authentically embrace our genuine selves, it is imperative to undertake a voyage of introspection and self-validation. This entails challenging the assumptions beneath conventional customs and pondering our personal principles, convictions, and ambitions. By closely analyzing the fronts we put up and how we conform, we can gradually disclose our real selves and promote more heartfelt connections.

Embrace your uniqueness, commemorate your special qualities, and value your viewpoints, hobbies, and wishes. Challenge the notion that conformity is necessary for acceptance. Meaningful connections grow from sincere self-expression, and it's essential to have relationships that allow for being seen as your true self, listening without judgment.

Practical Exercises for Fostering Authentic Connections with Others:

- **Active Listening: Engaging with Empathy**

    In our pursuit of authentic connections, one essential skill to cultivate is active listening. Active listening requires complete presence in conversations, engaging with others, and demonstrating empathy and understanding. Within this subsection, we will examine the value of active listening, strategies for implementing empathetic listening skills, and tactics for minimizing distractions to promote meaningful relationships.

    Active listening is like the superhero cape for building fun and authentic connections! The important thing is to display our authentic eagerness for others and construct a secure atmosphere where candid communication can flourish. Wearing our active listening gear signifies a dedication to values such as respect, empathy, and validation - the beautiful building blocks of creating meaningful bonds. Prepare yourself to don your superhero suit of active listening and witness the connections skyrocket to uncharted levels of awesomeness!

    To practice empathetic listening and validate others' experiences:

    Be Fully Present: Ensure that you are fully present and attentive when conversing in a chat, away from any sources of distraction, like smartphones or lingering thoughts. Show genuine interest through non-verbal cues like maintaining eye contact and nodding to encourage further sharing. These small actions motivate the other individual to continue spreading positive energy.

Show Empathy: Strive to grasp the emotions and viewpoints of the other party involved. Step into their perspective and imagine the emotional state they could be in. Avoid interrupting or offering immediate advice or solutions. Avoid any other strategy and concentrate on responding empathetically to validate their experiences. Let them know you understand by saying things like, 'I get why you might feel that way' or 'That sounds really difficult.'

Reflect and Clarify: Paraphrase and summarize what the person has shared to ensure accurate understanding. Showing reflection of their thoughts and feelings demonstrates your active listening skills and prompts them to dive deeper into their experiences. It appears that you're trying to convey...

Ask Open-Ended Questions: Motivate the individual to provide more details about their thoughts and emotions by posing open-ended inquiries. These questions prompt individuals to contemplate more profoundly and offer a platform to reveal further details about their experiences. For instance, inquire, 'What emotions did that circumstance evoke in you?' or 'Could you provide further details about the factors that influenced your choice?'

Manage Distractions: Minimize external and internal distractions during conversations. Disconnect from your electronic gadgets, discover a peaceful setting, and release any current worries from your mind. Develop a feeling of being fully present and concentrating on the individual and their words, enabling a more profound bond to develop.

Practicing active listening and demonstrating empathy enables us to build a conducive setting for fostering genuine bonds. Genuine understanding and validation lay the foundation for trust and meaningful relationships. By striving to be completely present and attentive during our interactions, we form more meaningful connections and display a sincere desire to build authentic relationships.

- **Sharing Vulnerabilities: Deepening Connections**

    Authentic connections are often built through acts of vulnerability, as they allow us to create deeper and more meaningful bonds. The vulnerability involves opening up and exposing our true selves, including our fears, insecurities, and personal experiences.

    Visualize vulnerability as a trusted comrade dedicated to skyrocketing your connections beyond ordinary limits! Embracing vulnerability has the power to invite extraordinary experiences into your life. The focus should be on generating chances for sincere connection, compassion, and comprehension. Opening up can create a chain reaction where others feel inspired and encouraged to share their stories. Picture it as constructing a superpower relationship, an interconnectedness, and commonality that will make you embody the essence of friendship's dynamic duo!

    To help you take your relationships on an epic adventure of shared experiences and heartfelt connections, here are a few tips to get you started:

1. Start Small: Begin by sharing less intimate aspects of your life, such as hobbies, interests, or favorite experiences. By testing the waters, you can gauge the level of comfort and trust within your relationship.

2. Express Emotions: Allow me to convey my emotions and impressions about particular circumstances or occurrences. This can assist in developing a more profound comprehension of your inner world and encourage others to share their feelings.

3. Share Personal Stories: Share personal stories that have gradually shaped you or influenced your perspectives. Sharing these stories can give others an understanding of your values, beliefs, and life experiences, fostering a deeper connection between you.

4. Practice Active Listening: Create a supportive atmosphere where individuals can freely share their vulnerabilities without concern for negative judgment. Implement the active listening techniques discussed earlier, showing empathy, validation, and genuine concern for their experiences.

5. Foster Reciprocity: Foster a culture of reciprocal vulnerability by showing understanding and support when others express their vulnerabilities. Foster an atmosphere where vulnerability is met with empathy and understanding. You foster a protected haven for more profound relationships to prosper by showcasing their importance and regard for emotional exposure.

Taking things slowly and being conscious of your comfort levels are vital to embracing vulnerability. It's unnecessary to share everything in one go – it's like stepping into the water cautiously and thoroughly immersing yourself later on. Once you locate a secure environment and muster the bravery, expressing your authentic feelings and encounters can help create deeper bonds with those around you.

Authenticity is key! Allowing your true essence to radiate creates an accepting ambiance that empowers others to do likewise. It's akin to a ripple effect of sincere bonds. Trust, understanding, and growth naturally flow when everyone feels safe to be themselves.

Settle down, inhale deeply, and open yourself up to the power of vulnerability. Bear in mind it's not about rushing forward recklessly. Take the happiness of forming valuable connections and watch your relationships blossom with understanding and authenticity.

Key Takeaways:

1. Developing authentic connections requires navigating societal expectations and overcoming barriers to authenticity.
2. Social expectations and masks can hinder our ability to express our true selves and form genuine connections.
3. Understanding attachment styles can shed light on our tendency to conform and the fear of rejection that may accompany it.
4. Active listening is a crucial skill in building authentic connections, involving being fully present, showing empathy, and validating others' experiences.
5. Vulnerability plays a transformative role in relationships, deepening connections and fostering trust.
6. Gradually sharing personal experiences and emotions can create a supportive environment for reciprocating vulnerability.
7. Building authentic connections takes time, trust, and a commitment to creating a safe space for open communication.

Now that we've explored developing authentic connections and overcoming barriers to authenticity, it's time to take action and apply this knowledge in your own life. The following action steps will guide you toward fostering genuine and meaningful connections with others.

1. Reflect on your attachment style: Take a moment to reflect on it and how it influences your behaviors and interactions in relationships. Understanding your attachment patterns will help you consciously navigate them and adjust as needed.

2. Reflect on your attachment style: Take a moment to reflect on it and how it influences your behaviors and interactions in relationships. Understanding your attachment patterns will help you consciously navigate them and adjust as needed.
3. Practice active listening: Make a conscious effort to engage in active listening during your conversations. Be fully present, show empathy, and validate the experiences of others. Incorporate active listening techniques such as reflecting, summarizing, and asking open-ended questions to deepen your understanding of others' perspectives.
4. Embrace vulnerability: Gradually open up and share aspects of your true self with others. Start by sharing less intimate experiences and emotions, and gradually work towards sharing more profound vulnerabilities. Remember to respect your boundaries and comfort levels while creating a supportive environment that encourages reciprocating vulnerability.
5. Cultivate a supportive network: Surround yourself with individuals who value authenticity and create a safe space for genuine connections. Seek out relationships where vulnerability is met with empathy and understanding. Nurture these connections by reciprocating vulnerability and actively listening to others.

In the next chapter, we will dive into the fascinating world of mindfulness and somatic practices and explore how they can enhance our ability to form authentic connections. Discover the power of being fully present at the moment, tuning into your body's wisdom, and cultivating deeper awareness in your interactions. Join us as we explore practical exercises and techniques that integrate mindfulness and somatic practices into your journey of developing authentic connections.

Integrating Mindfulness and Somatic Practices

Integrating mindfulness and somatic practices holds profound potential in healing attachment wounds and cultivating healthier relationships. This chapter talks about how these practices can change things a lot. It also studies how they help change attachments. When you use your current attention and listen to your body, you can start learning more about yourself, feeling better, and growing a lot.

Mindfulness Practices and Their Role in Attachment Transformation

Bringing your attention to the present moment on purpose is what mindfulness is about. We do it without judging and accepting. Practicing mindfulness teaches us to pay attention and feel better about our thoughts, feelings, and body. Recently, people started to appreciate mindfulness practices because they might make us feel better, lower our stress, and keep us healthy!

Mindfulness practices are essential to transform attachment. If we focus on the now, we can understand how we get attached to things. Our feelings and thoughts that make our relationships are called underlying emotions and beliefs. We can kindly observe our attachment-related thoughts, feelings, and actions when we practice mindfulness.

Panditharathne et al. conducted a study for the Journal of Personality and Social Psychology in 2015 and concluded that mindfulness meditation can increase self-awareness. The study participants who engaged in mindfulness meditation exhibited considerable advancements in self-awareness compared to the control group.

Through mindfulness, people can enhance their understanding of their emotions and recognize their personal necessities. Others' needs and emotions can become more familiar to them too. When they have a heightened awareness of themselves, it establishes a sturdy platform for understanding attachment dynamics and working towards healthier forms of connection. By cultivating mindfulness, we can free ourselves from unconscious reactions and gain the capacity to respond to relationship difficulties with intention, empathy, and understanding.

Furthermore, mindfulness exercises develop characteristics like acceptance, non-judgment, and compassion, which are crucial for healing attachment wounds. Individuals can develop a nurturing and supportive inner voice by cultivating self-compassion and fostering a secure internal base to explore and transform their attachment patterns.

Now actively doing attachment transformation work and integrating mindfulness exercises can give you an excellent idea of the strategy you need to adopt to improve your self-awareness, emotional regulation, and compassion. And once you get the hang of and understand the bigger picture, you can start fostering a secure attachment style and develop healthier relationships.

Next, we will explore mindfulness and somatic strategies that can bolster the process of transforming attachment. These practices present practical approaches and exercises to deepen self-awareness, control emotions, and nurture a secure bond.

Through involvement in these practices, people can initiate a transformative voyage of healing and expansion, forging a pathway towards more gratifying and nurturing relationships in their existence.

Mindfulness and Somatic Practices You Can Use

There are several things you can do to help transform your attachment issues or improve them. Below are some of the most helpful ones you can use and how they will help you.

- **Mindful Breathing**

    The practice of mindful breathing is essential in developing mindfulness and entails directing attention to the breath while observing it without judgment. By bringing attention to their breath, individuals can find stability in the present moment, regulate their emotions effectively, and embrace a feeling of tranquility. This practice enables individuals to enhance their self-regulation skills, empowering them to consciously and intentionally address attachment triggers instead of instinctively reacting based on previous experiences. 'The Effects of Mindful Breathing on Attachment Styles and Interpersonal Functioning,' a study by Jessica M. Bolger et al. in 2017, unveiled the positive impact of mindful breathing on attachment security and interpersonal functioning for adults with insecure attachment styles.

- **Body Scan**

    As mentioned earlier, Body scans are a gold mine! Practicing the body scan involves intentionally directing your awareness to different parts of your body and noticing any physical sensations, tension, or emotions that might arise. Practicing this technique allows you to develop a heightened sensitivity towards your body and establish a stronger relationship with your physical feelings. When you draw attention to your body, it can recognize areas of tension or unease that could potentially stem from attachment wounds. This enables you to release and heal these issues by practicing somatic awareness and showing compassion.

calmsage.com gives you a quick rundown on how to get going with body scan meditations:

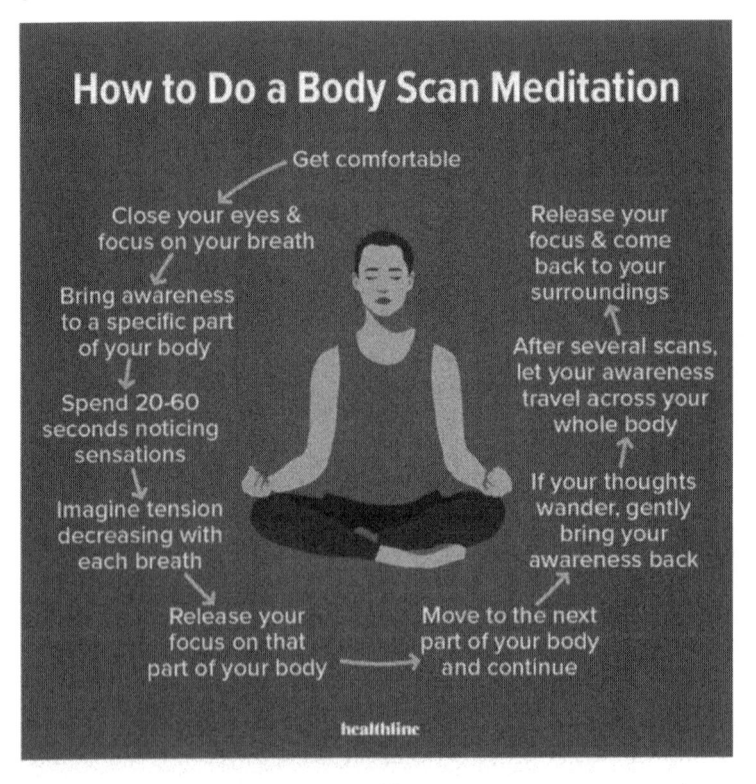

How to Do a Body Scan Meditation

- Get comfortable
- Close your eyes & focus on your breath
- Bring awareness to a specific part of your body
- Spend 20-60 seconds noticing sensations
- Imagine tension decreasing with each breath
- Release your focus on that part of your body
- Move to the next part of your body and continue
- If your thoughts wander, gently bring your awareness back
- After several scans, let your awareness travel across your whole body
- Release your focus & come back to your surroundings

healthline

(Source: Healthline.com)

- **Loving-Kindness Meditation**

    Loving-kindness meditation involves sending well-wishes and compassion to oneself and others. This practice cultivates a sense of connection, empathy, and kindness towards oneself and others, including attachment figures. By offering loving-kindness to oneself and visualizing sending it to attachment figures, individuals can nurture a sense of safety, healing, and forgiveness. The cultivation of secure attachment qualities like trust, compassion, and forgiveness is supported through this practice.

- **Yoga and Movement Practices**

    By incorporating the mind, body, and breath, yoga and other mindful movement practices offer a holistic way to transform attachments. These practices involve gentle, flowing movements, mindful breathing, and body awareness. Taking part in yoga or any form of mindful movement enables individuals to let go of bodily tension, establish a compassionate connection between their thoughts and physical state, and enhance self-awareness. Integrating the mind and body stimulates self-regulation, emotional restoration, and the nurturing of secure attachment traits. Insecurely attached adults can find solace from their anxiety and depression through yoga, according to a study conducted by Jessica M. Bolger et al. in 2015.

- **Somatic Experiencing**

    Somatic Experiencing is a therapy method that addresses trauma and attachment injuries by promoting somatic awareness. It involves gently exploring bodily sensations, movements, and gestures to release trapped energy and promote healing. Peter A. Levine and Ann Frederick in Asympathydy in 2014 found that Somatic Experiencing can effectively treat complex post-traumatic stress disorder (PTSD), often associated with insecure attachment styles. Somatic Experiencing assists individuals in cultivating a stronger feeling of safety and regulation within their physical bodies, enabling them to incorporate previous traumatic encounters and reform their attachments.

Mindfulness and somatic practices offer people potent resources to examine, heal, and reshape their attachment wounds. By assimilating these techniques into your everyday existence, you can foster self-awareness and regulate your emotions while nurturing traits like compassion and forgiveness. You will also learn to be more present in each moment. Through persistent dedication to practice, you can take a transformative path toward healing attachment wounds, leading to healthier and more fulfilling interactions with yourself and others.

Incorporating Somatic Techniques to Deepen Self-Awareness and Regulation

Adopting somatic techniques in your pursuit of personal growth and healing can bring about powerful transformations. The techniques appreciate that our body has clever thoughts and essential information. Understanding how our body senses, feelings, and thoughts can be achieved by first exploring this gateway. By purposefully tuning into the signals and sensations of our physical being we kickstart our adventure on the road, eager to unravel the mysteries within us and refine our self-command.

We can forget to listen to our body because the world is busy and exciting. The storm of thoughts and feelings can send us spinning. The critical components within our body often slip from our minds. Somatic techniques provide us with a means to reconnect with and actively listen to the language spoken by our bodies, unlocking doors that lead to an enhanced state of self-awareness.

Somatic practices enable us to become attuned and responsive and signs and bodily experiences that unfold within us. We notice how much energy we have and where it feels tight or loose. How we view our body during moments of presence. Through heightened self-awareness, we gain insight into how previous circumstances can shape our present reality and witness firsthand how emotional trauma from relationships can materialize physically.

As we deepen our self-awareness through somatic techniques, we also develop greater regulation over our emotions and responses. It's important to recognize how different emotions show up physically - for example, feeling a racing heart during moments of anxiety, experiencing tension in the jaw when angry, or sensing a weight on our chest when sadness takes hold. Through being mindful of these bodily feelings, we can acquire important awareness of our emotional terrain and intervene before our emotions become overpowering.

Implementing somatic techniques gives us tangible tools to regulate our emotions and uncover a sense of stability and relaxation. Grounding and centering practices enable us to stay fully present in the current moment, helping us root our energy and lay down a stable groundwork. Using breathing exercises and gentle movements allows us to appease our nervous system, inviting a state of tranquility and reestablishing a feeling of comfort within ourselves.

If that wasn't enough to get your bearings going, somatic techniques grant us means of expression and freedom. We can access the stored emotional energy through mindful movement and channel it into a beneficial expression. We respect our body's desire to let go by dancing, yoga, or other movements that express our feelings. Allowing for catharsis and transformation.

As we explore somatic methods on our path of personal growth and healing, we can discover newfound aspects of ourselves while building inner strength. We cultivate a deeper level of self-awareness, unlocking the body's wisdom and developing a greater understanding of our attachment wounds. By developing this increased awareness, we can better control our emotions, choose a thoughtful response instead of an impulsive reaction, and cultivate more positive and satisfying relationships.

How Exactly Do Somatic Techniques Help Deepen Self-Awareness and Emotional Regulation?

The study titled "Facilitating Adaptive Emotion Processing and Somatic Reappraisal via Sustained Mindful Interoceptive Attention" by Cynthia J. Price and Helen Y. Weng investigated the effects of sustained mindful interoceptive attention (SMIA) on adaptive emotion processing and somatic reappraisal. SMIA is a type of mindfulness meditation that involves paying attention to bodily sensations in a non-judgmental way.

The researchers found that SMIA led to improvements in both adaptive emotion processing and somatic reappraisal. Adaptive emotion processing is the ability to regulate emotions in a healthy way. Somatic reappraisal is the ability to change the meaning of bodily sensations in a way that is less distressing.

Here is a chart that shows where mindfulness and somatic experiencing come into play:

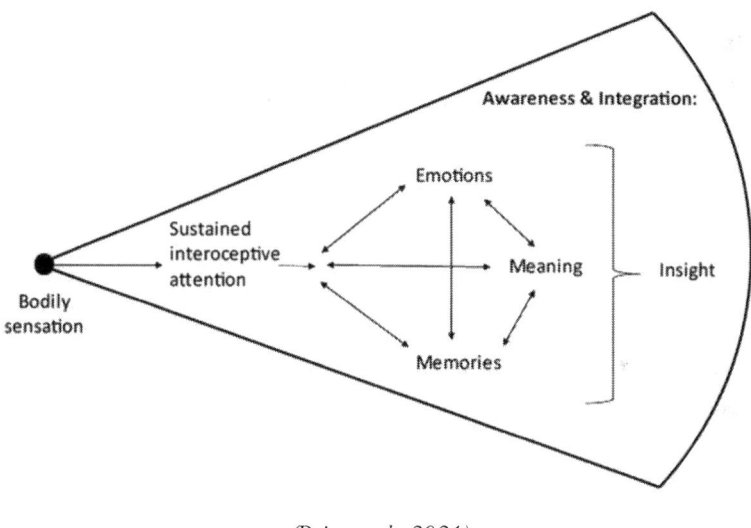

(Price et al., 2021)

- **Body Sensations Awareness:**

    Utilizing somatic techniques directs individuals' attention toward the nuanced and refined sensations experienced in their bodies. Through practicing body awareness, individuals can uncover valuable information about how their emotions and attachment styles manifest in tangible ways. For instance, you can sense tightness in the chest when undergoing anxiety or experience a heavy feeling in the stomach during sadness. Developing a heightened understanding of oneself allows people to identify and track their emotional experiences, empowering them to meet their needs with conscious thoughtfulness.

- **Grounding and Centering Practices:**

    Connecting with the present moment and cultivating an internal sense of stability are primary objectives achieved through grounding and centering exercises incorporated into somatic techniques. A third option is to bring awareness to how the body's weight feels against a supportive surface. Grounding and centering allow individuals to stay present and control their emotions, mitigating overwhelming feelings or detachment typically experienced with attachment wounds.

- **Body-Based Regulation Techniques:**

    Somatic techniques offer various tools for self-regulation. Adopting these methods can support individuals in moving from states of distress or disregulation toward a more harmonious and peaceful state. Deep breathing exercises, progressive muscle relaxation, and gentle movements are examples of body-based regulation techniques used to promote relaxation and release tension. Through these methods, people can successfully ease their nervous system, lower anxiety levels, and restore a sense of salves.

- **Expressive Movement and Release:**

  Somatic techniques allow you to express and release pent-up emotions stored in the body. Incorporating movement techniques like shaking, stretching, or dancing into your routine can unlock your inner potential for self-expression and release any emotional tension in your physical being. This process allows for a cathartic experience and supports the release of stored trauma or attachment-related wounds, fostering healing and integration.

- **Body-Informed Decision-Making:**

  Incorporating somatic techniques into decision-making processes can enhance self-awareness and ensure choices align with one's authentic needs and values. By tuning into the body's sensations, individuals can attune to the subtle cues and signals that arise when faced with decisions or relationship dynamics. This body-informed approach helps individuals navigate situations from a place of embodied wisdom, fostering healthier choices and more aligned actions.

Incorporating somatic techniques into daily life can deepen self-awareness and regulation, empowering individuals to navigate attachment wounds with greater ease and resilience. These techniques offer a profound understanding of the mind-body connection and provide practical tools for healing, growth, and transformation. By integrating somatic practices, individuals can cultivate a more profound self-awareness, regulate their emotions more effectively, and foster greater empowerment and well-being.

Mindfulness And Somatic Exercises for Enhancing Attachment Security

As we've established in this chapter, mindfulness and somatic exercises offer valuable tools for enhancing attachment security and fostering healthier and more secure relationships. Through developing presence, self-consciousness, and sensitivity towards our bodily experiences, we can confront and mend attachment scars, encourage emotional stability, and establish a secure base within ourselves and our interactions with others.

R.A.I.N

First, let's talk about a little girl I came to know. Let's call her Emma for the sake of this book. Emma was a child abuse and neglect victim, with gashes and scars all over her body as she grew older. She often wore clothes to hide them and never talked about anything as a teenager. This disrupted her school life as well as her social endeavors. Emma was referred to a professional who insisted she tries the R.A.I.N technique. And so she did. The results were astounding. Not only did her self-image improve, her grades did as well. She said the technique helped her "talk" about her trauma without feeling judged. She also said that it helped her to "process" her trauma and to "heal."

The R.A.I.N. technique can greatly improve our attachment security by offering a structure for dealing with our emotions and patterns linked to attachment. The acronym R.A.I.N. represents four key steps: Recognize, Allow, Investigate, and Nurture. These steps provide distinct chances for both healing and personal development. Here are 4 steps that can be followed to use this technique:

Integrating Mindfulness and Somatic Practices

1. Before taking any other action, we must acknowledge our sentiments and conduct concerning attachment. To know when we feel insecure scared of being left alone, or acting anxiously or avoidantly because of attachment-related triggers; we must watch ourselves and be very aware. It suggests that we must diligently cultivate mindfulness toward our thoughts and emotions. We can make these feelings and behaviors clearer by using a light and recognizing that they are there.

2. You can now let these emotions and patterns exist without passing any judgment. This requires creating a safe and accepting space within ourselves to fully experience and explore these attachment-related feelings. We don't halt or overlook our emotions; we permit them to manifest and acknowledge them with a gentle and understanding mindset. Doing this lets us be kind and calm about our hurts from being attached. We can help ourselves feel better by being kind and understanding to ourselves.

3. Investigate's third step invites us to explore the underlying beliefs and needs contributing to our attachment patterns. This requires us to explore our innermost thoughts, convictions, and stories about ourselves and our connections. Through analyzing these underlying assumptions and yearnings, we can gain valuable insights into the causes of our attachment scars and how they shape our current experiences. This investigation process allows us to challenge and reframe negative or limiting beliefs, fostering a more secure and empowering attachment narrative.

4. During the last step, called Nurture, we prioritize offering ourselves kindness, compassion, and self-care in response to our attachment wounds. Creating a caring and supportive internal atmosphere is crucial to avoid negative feelings about ourselves when we encounter obstacles in developing close connections with others. We learn to be kind to ourselves like we would be kind to someone we love by practicing self-compassion. Being caring helps you get better and bigger. Feeling confident and having fewer concerns can enhance the strength of our relationships.

In an article written for mindful.org, Tara Brach talks about her experiences with R.A.I.N.

"When I was in college, I went off to the mountains for a weekend of hiking with an older, wiser friend of twenty-two. After setting up our tent, we sat by a stream, watching the water swirl around rocks, talking about our lives. At one point, she described how she was learning to be "her own best friend." A wave of sadness came over me, and I broke down sobbing. I was the furthest thing from my own best friend. I was continually harassed by an inner judge who was merciless, nit-picking, demanding, and always on the job. My guiding assumption was, "Something is fundamentally wrong with me," as I struggled to control and fix what felt like a flawed self."

"Over the last several decades, through my work with tens of thousands of clients and meditation students, I've come to see the pain of perceived deficiency as an epidemic. It's like we're in a trance that causes us to see ourselves as unworthy. Yet, I have seen in my own life and countless others that we can awaken from this trance through practicing mindfulness and self-compassion. We can come to trust the goodness and purity of our hearts."

She uses this image to describe the technique:

Feeling Overwhelmed?
Remember "RAIN"
Four steps to stop being so hard on ourselves.

R A I N

R — Recognize what's going on

A — Allow the experience to be there, just as it is

I — Investigate with kindness

N — Natural awareness, which comes from not identifying with the experience

(Source: mindful.org)

Somatic Exercises

Exercises such as body scans and body awareness practices I've mentioned above are also instrumental in enhancing attachment security. These exercises encompass concentrating on your body's sensory feedback and fostering a sense of protection, serenity, and connectivity. Through connecting with the experiences happening within us physically, we amplify our connection with our wants and emotions, which helps us regulate ourselves and cultivate a solid emotional core.

Breathing exercises

They are precious for promoting attachment security. Utilizing deep belly or coherent breathing practices can regulate your nervous system, diminish anxiety symptoms, and create a tranquil state. Regularly participating in these exercises can foster the skill of soothing ourselves and controlling our emotions. This, in turn, boosts our feelings of security and encourages more secure attachment behaviors within our relationships.

Mindful communication

Enhancing attachment security involves considering this important aspect as well. Through dedicated practice in attentive listening and expressive speaking, we can learn to be fully present in interactions while comprehending both personal feelings and the feelings of others. Expressing oneself in this manner cultivates understanding and compassion within individuals. We are dedicated to forming protective, trustworthy, and supportive relationships. Mindful communication also helps us recognize and navigate attachment triggers, facilitating healthier and more secure relational dynamics.

Self-compassion

Enhancing attachment security requires the cultivation of self-compassion using mindfulness and somatic practices. By developing a kind and nurturing relationship with ourselves, we heal attachment wounds, reduce self-criticism, and cultivate a secure internal base. Practicing self-kindness through meditation allows us to fill gaps in the love and care we received during our formative years. It's called mindful self-compassion! Feeling confident and having self-compassion can enhance your resilience. Building a firm groundwork allows you to establish secure attachments in relationships.

Incorporating mindfulness and somatic exercises into our lives can significantly enhance attachment security and transform our relationship dynamics. Through these activities, we can enhance self-awareness, manage our feelings effectively, and show compassion towards ourselves. Establishing a strong bond requires the presence of these vital factors. Placing emphasis on internal emotions, attuning ourselves to bodily cues, and maintaining a state of mindfulness allows us to make strides in self-development. We prioritize safety and take measures to establish a robust security framework that not only protects us but also safeguards our friends. Continuously implementing these practices can lead to substantial changes in our attachment patterns. Having healthy, satisfying, and safe relationships comes from this.

Key Takeaways:

1. Mindfulness and somatic practices are powerful tools for healing attachment wounds and promoting attachment transformation.

2. Somatic techniques focus on the body's wisdom and the connection between physical sensations, emotions, and thoughts, allowing for deeper self-awareness and regulation.

3. The R.A.I.N. technique (Recognize, Allow, Investigate, Nurture) is a mindfulness practice that can enhance attachment security by cultivating compassion and non-reactivity toward attachment wounds.

4. Mindfulness and somatic exercises help individuals access their inner wisdom, regulate emotions, and better understand their attachment patterns and needs.

5. By incorporating somatic techniques into personal growth and healing journeys, individuals can deepen self-awareness, regulate emotions, and foster healing from attachment wounds.

6. Integrating mindfulness and somatic practices promote self-compassion, self-acceptance, and a stronger sense of self-worth in attachment.

7. These practices empower individuals to develop healthier attachment dynamics, cultivate secure relationships, and experience greater well-being.

Call to Action Steps:

- Start incorporating mindfulness into your daily routine by setting aside a few minutes each day for meditation, deep breathing, or body awareness exercises. Begin with just a few minutes and gradually increase the duration as you become more comfortable.

- Explore somatic practices such as body scans, yoga, or tai chi. Find a class or online resource that resonates with you and commit to practicing regularly. Pay attention to how these practices help you connect with your body and cultivate a sense of embodiment.

- Experiment with the R.A.I.N. technique during emotional distress or when attachment-related patterns arise. Take a pause, recognize and name the emotions you are experiencing, allow them to be present without judgment, investigate the underlying beliefs or needs that may be driving them, and nurture yourself with self-compassion and self-care.

- Consider working with a trained therapist specializing in attachment and somatic approaches. A therapist can provide guidance, support, and personalized techniques to help you navigate and heal attachment wounds.

- Keep a journal to reflect on your experiences, insights, and progress in integrating mindfulness and somatic practices into your attachment healing journey. Use the journal for self-reflection, tracking patterns, and celebrating growth.

- Seek additional resources, books, and workshops on mindfulness, somatic practices, and attachment theory to deepen your understanding and continue your personal growth.

Remember, healing attachment wounds is a process that requires patience, self-compassion, and dedication. By taking these actionable steps, you are actively investing in your well-being and creating the opportunity for transformation and greater attachment security.

Nurturing Self-Compassion

"Self-compassion is simply giving the same kindness to ourselves that we would give to others." - Christopher Germer.

At times, we become so absorbed in forming connections with others that we overlook our most vital relationship with ourselves. The main element is the cultivation of sincere self-compassion. Regard it as the special spice that enables sincere connections to blossom!

A magical transformation occurs when we show kindness, understanding, and forgiveness to ourselves. We start extending that same goodness to others. It's like a ripple effect of awesomeness! The foundation of self-compassion showcases vulnerability, authenticity, and empathy. And that's when our partnerships move from ordinary to astonishing!

So Hey, how about dedicating some time to nurture your self-compassion? Show yourself kindness, ease off on self-criticism, and observe as your potential for developing profound and meaningful bonds shoots up. The key factor is building a vibe of comprehension and empathy, contributing to flourishing and fulfilling relationships.

In this chapter, we will investigate the transforming influence of self-compassion. In attachment relationships, we will acquire useful techniques and practices to nurture them. Gear up for an expedition of self-discovery and cultivating self-empathy, creating opportunities for authentic connections with others.

Importance of Self-Compassion in Building Healthy Relationships:

- **Fostering self-compassion as a foundation for connection.**

    Having a solid grounding in self-compassion is crucial for cultivating positive and genuine bonds. Nurturing a compassionate relationship with ourselves empowers us to establish a realm of love, acceptance, and comprehension. This space enables our connections with others to grow.

    Scientific research indicates that incorporating self-compassion into our lives is akin to having a hidden ingredient for nurturing secure attachment styles. The focus lies in satisfying our own emotional requirements and experiencing a sense of inner security and validation. And guess what? This bolsters our assurance and readiness to be sincere in relationships!

    But here's the cool part: Self-compassion extends beyond benefiting only ourselves. A magical transformation takes place when we wholeheartedly embrace our vulnerabilities and imperfections. Our understanding and empathy for the challenges and humanness of those nearby deepens. It's like wearing empathy glasses! Such heightened empathy cultivates stronger ties and amplifies the fantastic relationships we develop with others.

    By showing ourselves a little love, we look after our well-being and generate a ripple effect of comprehension and compassion that enhances our connections with others. Be prepared to develop rock-solid attachments and build relationships encompassing compassion, empathy, and authentic connection!

Additionally, self-compassion safeguards against unavoidable barriers and conflicts within relationships. It supports us in navigating tough situations with gentleness and understanding. It decreases the chance of participating in harmful patterns of blame or criticism. By cultivating kindness and understanding within ourselves, we develop a greater capacity to demonstrate these qualities toward our partners, friends, and loved ones.

How do we do it? Well, it's pretty simple. We must remember the significance of dedicating time to acknowledge our feelings, assess our deeds, and just take a break to unwind. We've got this! When we extend kindness towards ourselves and delve into our true essence, it has a transformative impact on our relationships with others.

It's like magic! When we show ourselves kindness, everything transforms. Becoming more open and authentic enhances the dynamics of our friendships by attracting an abundance of good vibes. Let's begin by showing kindness to ourselves and witnessing how our relationships with others reach an extraordinary level of greatness!

- **Embracing imperfections and fostering acceptance**

  In a culture that often idolizes flawless standards, it can pose difficult to completely embrace our authentic selves. Nevertheless, embracing our flaws and self-approval is crucial in establishing genuine and satisfying connections.

By extending sincere kindness and empathy to ourselves, we construct a welcoming and supportive haven within our beings. Don't forget that we are all human, my amigo. Imperfections are a natural part of being human and shouldn't define our worth. It's all included in the gig. So, let's release that self-criticism and make room for self-kindness and self-love instead.

Here's the thing: Magic occurs when we accept and celebrate our imperfections. We can stop chasing this unrealistic idea of perfection and be authentic. Authenticity and vulnerability are essential. And you know what? That vulnerability deepens our connections with others. They can relate to the whole imperfection thing too! It's reminiscent of discovering common interests and cultivating authentic bonds.

So, why not leave behind self-judgment and wholeheartedly accept the uniqueness of being perfectly flawed? By showing ourselves serious kindness, we create space for authenticity and connection in our relationships. Authenticity and reliability are what matter, my friend!

This process depends on self-compassion. Increasing our self-kindness can lead to a higher likelihood of demonstrating kindness toward others. By accepting our authentic selves, we can cultivate an environment of empathy and acceptance toward others in our relationships.

Additionally, nurturing self-compassion strengthens our capability to embrace vulnerability. By displaying self-compassion towards ourselves, we construct a protective zone within us where we can delve into our emotions. We also disclose our genuine selves to others. This vulnerability forms the bedrock for heartfelt connections. We let others observe us completely, flaws and all.

We invite greater authenticity into our relationships by embracing imperfections and fostering self-acceptance. We release the pressure to meet impossible standards and instead focus on cultivating meaningful connections based on genuine acceptance and understanding. By starting this adventure of self-compassion and self-acceptance, we equip ourselves to show up completely and genuinely in our relationships, creating settings where true connection can prosper.

- **Fostering Empathy and Understanding**

    Being gentle with ourselves aids in our comprehension of and empathy towards others. We can understand our weaknesses, problems, and mistakes without blaming ourselves with self-compassion. We must treat others without judgment, mirroring how we approach ourselves.

    When we show compassion towards ourselves and attain a deep comprehension of our own feelings, desires, and thoughts, it allows us to better empathize with the emotions experienced by others. Increasing our knowledge helps us see the similarities between us more clearly. We all feel pain, happiness, and worries. Empathy rests upon understanding. We can understand what others go through and help them without being mean.

    By practicing self-kindness in our relationships, we construct a supportive setting for genuine expression and embracing feelings. We ensure the safety and acceptance of everyone. When we display our genuine selves, it assists others in feeling at ease to do likewise. Cultivating trust in others involves showing empathy and genuinely understanding their feelings. We grow even closer.

Additionally, showing yourself kindness can shield you from experiencing negative emotions and damaging valuable friendships. let's rock that self-kindness, manage those insecurities like a boss, and keep those friendships strong. When we approach situations with kindness, it benefits everyone involved. Gear up to build a pleasant and amicable ambiance that enables everyone to thrive and establish profound relationships.

Techniques for Cultivating Self-Compassion and Self-Acceptance:

- **Mindfulness practices for self-compassion**

  In this hectic world, stumbling upon moments of tranquility and awareness can transform our lives. Intentionally bringing our attention to the present moment with acceptance and without criticism - is what mindfulness entails. It is an effective practice for fostering self-compassion.

  Engaging in self-compassion meditations is a crucial mindfulness strategy for fostering self-compassion. These meditations involve directing loving-kindness and compassion towards ourselves. By being gently guided, we discover how to acknowledge our challenges, show empathy, and realize our inherent worthiness of love and acceptance.

Mindfulness involves focusing on our inner world and merely noticing our emotions without becoming entangled or striving to modify them. Imagine yourself as an emotion detective, you know?

Something remarkable unfolds when we start to recognize and acknowledge our emotional landscape. Responding with greater understanding and kindness towards ourselves is important. It's like embracing ourselves tightly in times of utmost need. Recognizing the value in allowing ourselves to feel, we make space for our emotions just as we would extend it to a friend who seeks comfort. When those emotions appear, we will offer ourselves heartfelt self-compassion, like we would extend to a trusted companion.

Including self-compassionate self-talk in your mindfulness routine can bring about powerful results. It encompasses deliberately altering our internal monologue from self-blame to self-care. Once we realize the negative and critical language we use towards ourselves, we can intentionally substitute it with compassionate, empowering, and uplifting words. Practicing this can assist us in fostering a gentle and understanding internal narrative.

Engaging in mindfulness activities for self-care allows us to acquire some incredibly fascinating knowledge. We're talking about three important things: Noticing aspects, being content with them, and showing ourselves sincere love.

Through mindfulness, we unlock superhuman abilities to notice our thoughts, emotions, and actions attentively. It's like gaining expertise in observing our own minds. We can truly comprehend ourselves deeper and act according to our unique preferences.

And let me tell you, it's awe-inspiring! Feeling accepted begins when we wholeheartedly embrace the present moment and its joys and challenges. Rather than passing judgment or opposing, we are gracefully surrendering to the current. It feels like applauding ourselves for being authentic.

But wait, there's more! Consider mindfulness as an intensive course in treating yourself with kindness. As we progress in life, we understand the importance of practicing immense kindness, nurturing ourselves, and treating ourselves with the utmost care, just like how we treat someone dear to us. The essence lies in practicing self-love and compassion, my amigo.

We can make self-kindness grow by doing mindful things every day. Utilizing these activities enables us to have some downtime, build a connection with ourselves as friends, and adeptly manage our internal feelings. As we learn about mindfulness and cultivate self-compassion, our sense of self grows stronger. We can love and accept ourselves too.

- **Challenging self-critical thoughts and fostering self-acceptance:**

    We possess an internal voice that can occasionally be harsh and judgmental. Just think about the potential of converting that voice into a gentle and accepting one. We can foster a more understanding connection with ourselves by challenging the negativity in our minds and promoting self-acceptance.

A powerful technique is employing self-compassionate language. It entails intentionally opting for gentle and supportive language. Rather than being hard on ourselves for our errors, we can offer kind and empathetic words when we make mistakes. "I can gain knowledge from this incident and evolve." By utilizing language that shows kindness towards ourselves, we transform our internal dialogue into one that fosters self-acceptance and progress.

Another powerful technique is to reframe negative self-talk. The process includes confronting and changing pessimistic thoughts with optimistic and practical ones. If we notice ourselves engaging in self-criticism, it can actually be helpful: instead of dwelling on the notion that one is a failure, it is possible to reinterpret it as follows - 'I encountered a difficult situation, but I approached it with determination, and that's what matters.' By reframing our thoughts in this manner, we can nurture self-acceptance and acknowledge our efforts toward personal growth.

Fostering self-acceptance also requires practicing self-forgiveness. The collective group of individuals, including ourselves, possesses the quality of imperfection and a proclivity for making mistakes. Acknowledging our faults, assuming the blame for them, and forgiving ourselves is crucial. By granting ourselves forgiveness, we liberate ourselves from the heaviness of guilt and self-reproach, empowering us to advance with self-care and individual progress.

We can practice practical exercises to integrate these techniques into our everyday activities. One exercise is keeping a self-compassion journal, where we write down self-compassionate statements and positive affirmations. Besides that, it is within our power to recognize habitual negative thoughts about ourselves and actively reframe them with positive and compassionate alternatives. Through consistent dedication to these exercises, we progressively reframe our thoughts and foster a mindset characterized by self-acceptance.

Bear in mind promoting self-acceptance is an expedition that demands patience and practice. Encountering obstacles is to be expected on the path, but through commitment and showing kindness to oneself, we can attain considerable growth. To cultivate a nurturing environment within us that cultivates self-acceptance, we must address our own critical thoughts head-on and replace them with compassionate ones. Additionally, reframing negative inner dialogues and practicing forgiveness towards oneself are crucial elements in this process. This enables authentic connections and a more fulfilling existence.

Self-Reflective Exercises for Developing Self-Compassion in Attachment Relationships

- **Exploring attachment history and self-compassion**

  Our attachment history greatly impacts how we perceive ourselves and our relationships. How we have attached in the past greatly influences our capacity to cultivate self-compassion. Through a closer examination of our attachment experiences, we can gain valuable insights into how they have affected our perception of ourselves, our tendency to critique ourselves, and our capacity to show compassion.

Let's kickstart this journey of self-discovery with a fun and reflective exercise: journaling! Get your preferred notebook and allocate some time to explore your attachment history.

Allow your thoughts and memories to flow onto those pages, my beloved friend. Reflect on those early attachment experiences and relationships that have shaped you. Ponder on the characteristics of those relationships - were they capable of offering you the emotional support and validation you sought? Could you share your feelings during those interactions?

And here's the juicy part: consider how these experiences may have influenced your beliefs about yourself. Do you feel deserving of both love and acceptance in every aspect? Let those reflections flow and see what insights and discoveries come up.

Remember, this journaling adventure is all about exploring and understanding yourself better. Give yourself permission to let your pen effortlessly flow across the pages, exposing the intricate layers of your personal history with attachments.

As you explore your past attachments further, you might start recognizing patterns in how you perceive yourself and criticize yourself. Maybe you tend to be overly critical of yourself because you lacked emotional understanding in your early relationships. In case you struggle with emotions of not deserving and fear of rejection due to previous encounters with caregivers who lacked consistency or trustworthiness... Acknowledging these patterns enables you to better grasp how your attachment history has molded your path toward developing self-compassion.

Self-inquiry prompts can be valuable tools in this process. Consider questions such as:

1. How have my early attachment experiences influenced my self-perception and beliefs about myself?
2. In what ways do I tend to be self-critical, and how might this relate to my attachment history?
3. Are there any particular attachment-related fears or insecurities that impact my ability to practice self-compassion?
4. How can I bring more self-compassion to the wounded parts of myself that emerged from my attachment experiences?

As we involve ourselves in these reflective tasks, we develop a stronger understanding of the connection between our past attachments and our ability to extend self-love. Recognizing the impact of our past experiences allows us to acknowledge how they have shaped our internal conversations, how we perceive ourselves, and how we extend compassion towards ourselves.

Don't forget approaching this exploration demands being gentle and having self-compassion towards oneself. A curious and open mindset is crucial when doing these exercises, enabling us to discover insights without blaming or criticizing ourselves. By illuminating our attachment history, we unlock

- **Practicing self-compassion in attachment challenges:**

    the potential for healing, progress, and fostering of self-compassion within our attachment bonds and beyond.

    In attachment relationships, challenges like triggers, conflicts, and communication difficulties are commonplace. One effective method for developing understanding, empathy, and kindness in ourselves and our relationships is to approach these challenges with self-compassion.

    Envision being a compassionate friend who extends support and understanding to others grappling with attachment struggles that mirror your own.

    Consider the thoughtful phrases and meaningful actions you would share with this beloved friend. In what ways can you express sympathy and goodwill towards them? Take a brief pause to note down these understanding replies, capturing the gentleness and supportiveness you would show towards them.

    Here's the magical part: turn those kind words and gestures inward. If you encounter comparable difficulties and obstacles on your attachment journey, implement these methods yourself. Treat yourself as you would that dear friend, showering yourself with empathy and kindness. Prioritize self-compassion while navigating through your attachment journeys. By treating ourselves as we would a dear friend, we bring self-compassion into the heart of our attachment challenges.

A beneficial method involves incorporating self-compassionate self-talk into moments of conflict or situations that cause distress. Stop momentarily when encountering a demanding interaction and remind yourself that experiencing relationship difficulties is normal. Offer yourself understanding and reassurance through affirmations like "I'm giving my best in this situation" or "It's wonderful to feel upset or triggered at the moment." You build a supportive inner narrative that fosters personal growth and empathy by acknowledging your compassion.

In attachment relationships, facing communication challenges is quite common. When facing misunderstandings or conflicts, incorporating self-compassion can be transformative. Start by recognizing and embracing your emotions, reminding yourself that having varying needs and viewpoints is normal. Cultivate active listening by being fully present with your inner experiences and the other person, embracing an open-hearted and non-judgmental stance. Respond with kindness and empathy, aiming to understand their perspective rather than jumping to defensiveness or criticism. We promote a culture of compassion and teamwork by addressing communication hurdles with self-compassion.

Remember, the journey of practicing self-compassion in attachment challenges is ongoing. The main point is not about achieving perfection or never making mistakes; it's about embracing ourselves and our connections with kindness, empathy, and an openness to learn from our experiences. By infusing these exercises into our regular routines, we empower ourselves to navigate attachment-related difficulties by embracing self-compassion. This process facilitates the development of deeper understanding and promotes authentic internal and external connections.

> **Key takeaways:**
>
> 1. Building healthy relationships requires self-compassion. Developing genuine connections with others starts by cultivating self-compassion. We are kind and understanding towards ourselves when we create a nurturing environment that supports the growth of healthy relationships.
>
> 2. Practicing self-compassion by embracing imperfections and fostering self-acceptance, including kindness and understanding towards ourselves, is crucial. By releasing self-judgment and embracing our true selves, we improve our capacity for vulnerability and authenticity in relationships.
>
> 3. Mindfulness practices aid in developing self-compassion: Mindfulness techniques supply helpful strategies for nurturing self-compassion. We foster heightened awareness, acceptance, and kindness toward ourselves by implementing self-compassion meditations, being mindful of our emotions, and practicing self-compassionate inner dialogue.
>
> 4. We can foster self-acceptance by challenging self-critical thoughts and reframing negative self-talk; by incorporating self-compassionate language, shifting negative thoughts, and implementing self-forgiveness practices, we generate a more nurturing and compassionate inner conversation.

5. The way we view ourselves, critique ourselves, and practice self-compassion is influenced by our attachment history. By taking part in self-reflective exercises and self-inquiry, we acquire insights into how our journey toward self-compassion has been molded by our early attachment experiences.

6. In attachment challenges, practicing self-compassion. Utilizing self-compassion in attachment relationships enables us to effectively navigate challenges like triggers, conflict, and difficulties in communication. By showing ourselves kindness, empathy, and understanding, we develop a compassionate and supportive approach to challenges associated with attachment.

By fostering self-compassion using these measures, you establish a groundwork for building authentic connections in your life. The next chapter will investigate merging mindfulness and somatic practices, enriching our path toward forming meaningful bonds.

Enhancing Relationship Skills

"Communication is the solvent of all problems and is the foundation for personal development." - Peter Shepherd

Many people often don't realize how their relationships suffer from simple failures in communication. This quote by Peter Shepherd very eloquently highlights the transformative power hidden within being able to communicate effectively with the people you care so deeply about.

Just imagine a world where every conversation felt like a deep connection, where conflicts were transformed into opportunities for growth. Doesn't that sound amazing? When you have a solid ability to connect with the people around you, you can very quickly lay the groundwork for establishing a secure connection, so in this chapter, In this section, you will uncover the solution to activating this revolutionary skill.

You will also learn efficient techniques to transform how you convey yourself, handle disagreements, and cultivate bonds. Prepare yourself as you move forward because you may not even recognize yourself by the end!

Effective Communication Strategies for Building Secure Attachments:

I think it's safe to say that communication is a 2-way thing, so before I dive into how you can express yourself, let's turn our heads (and ears) towards who we want to communicate with and practice a little thing known as active listening.

- **Active Listening:**

    In any attachment, one of the most fundamental and powerful skills you can develop is active listening. It is as simple as talking less and listening more! And it's not just simply hearing the words spoken; it involves fully engaging with whoever you are communicating with, understanding their perspective, and validating their feelings. A couple of sentences at a time with a gap in between to let them respond and elaborate.

    Researchers at Wright State University totally agree with me on this one. A study of 100 managers and employees of a large hospital system showed that effective listeners were likelier to have high-performing teams and be seen as influential leaders. It further showed that active listening can increase trust, reduce conflict, and improve relationship motivation.

    Remember that you shouldn't just disconnect from the conversation and only hop in when you think you should. Instead, give them your undivided attention. Put away your phone, turn off the TV, and create a quiet and uninterrupted space where you are at the center.

    If you actively listen, you display respect, empathy, and a genuine curiosity in grasping the thoughts and feelings of the other person. Such awareness enhances the connection among you both and stimulates the other person to respond with a similar enthusiasm.

    A tip that might help you keep going is to reflect on what they have said and paraphrase it while adding a bit of your own. This not only ensures that you have understood what the other person is saying but it confirms for the other person that you are there in the moment with them. This is an essential cornerstone in building a secure attachment.

You could then further go on by acknowledging and validating their feelings. This expresses empathy, and even if you may not fully agree or share the same emotions, validating them helps them feel heard, strengthening your trust and emotional connection.

- **Nonverbal Communication**

Now, communication is not limited to words alone. Communication is not limited to words. In fact, a significant portion of our messages is conveyed through nonverbal cues, such as body language, facial expressions, tone of voice, and gestures. The little sprinkle on top seals the deal in the other person's head that you are there with them.

Now this isn't just about making eye contact (although that's important too). It's about your posture and body alignment, gestures and movement, and of course, your little facial expressions.

Fun Fact: Around 70% of all communication is nonverbal! This chart created by Amutan et al. shows just that.

VERBAL 35%

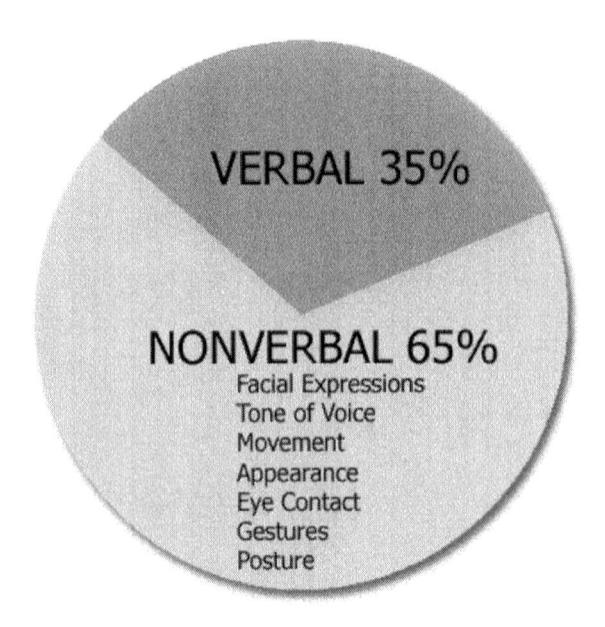

NONVERBAL 65%
Facial Expressions
Tone of Voice
Movement
Appearance
Eye Contact
Gestures
Posture

(Amutan et al, 2017)

Here's how each of them plays a part and how you can keep them in check:

Posture and Body Alignment: It's essential to be attentive and look attentive. Maintain an open and upright posture, and don't cross your arms or legs, as this can make you seem closed off and unwilling to be vulnerable.

Eye Contact: As always, this is one of the most essential things when attempting to communicate effectively. This conveys that you are attentive, engaged, and responsive during a conversation. But remember to consider cultural differences and personal preferences for eye contact.

Facial Expressions: The face is a powerful tool for expressing emotions. Keep an eye on your facial expressions and use them to convey your true feelings. A pleasant and inviting atmosphere may be created by passing a quick smile occasionally, for example.

Gestures and Movement: Making deliberate, appropriate gestures can significantly aid in getting your message across. But remember to pay attention to excessive or disruptive behavior since it may undermine your message.

- **Assertive Expression**

Now, this is another essential skill, but it's all about you (well, mostly) this time. Picture this: A relationship where both parties feel heard and respected! Sounds pretty lovely if you ask me. But how?

You see, having assertiveness allows you to express yourself with self-assurance. Instead of beating around the bush or even resorting to passive-aggressive communication styles, assertiveness empowers you to voice your necessities, aspirations, and limits in a straightforward yet polite way. Doing so creates a safe space for open conversation and avoids misinterpretations from clouding your bond. This aims to establish a foundation of clear and open dialogue that clears the path for sound and balanced connections.

Having set the significance of assertiveness, let's examine some valuable methods for expressing oneself clearly:

Use "I" statements rather than "you" at the beginning of your sentences to convey your views and feelings without coming off as accusing. This slight change in terminology encourages open communication and enables you to accept responsibility for your feelings.

Be Concrete and Specific: To help your spouse better understand your requirements, wants, or limits, provide specific examples when expressing them. Being clear and concise lowers the possibility of misunderstanding and ensures your message is correctly understood.

Active listening and empathy exercises should be done when your spouse shares their needs or boundaries. Give them your attention, demonstrate empathy, and ask questions to help them understand more. This encourages open communication and cultivates a climate of mutual respect.

Look for Win-Win Solutions: Approach arguments or disagreements from a team perspective. Rather than concentrating on winning or losing, try to find solutions that consider bur your spouse's needs. This collaborative strategy strengthens your bond and encourages dialogue.

Adopt an Assertive Voice: Adopting an assertive voice may seem strange initially, but with practice, it will become a natural tool in your communication toolbox. Keep in mind that you deserve to have your choices and ideas respected. Adopting an assertive voice lays the groundwork for better communication, greater comprehension, and fulfilling interactions.

Now that we have explored the essential foundation of effective communication strategies for building secure attachments let's focus on another critical aspect of nurturing healthy relationships: conflict resolution. While effective communication helps us establish strong connections, conflicts are inevitable in any relationship. The key lies in how we navigate and resolve them\

Conflict Resolution Techniques for Healthier Relationship Dynamics

Now, conflicts are a natural part of any relationship and don't have to be bad. In fact, I would argue that it is healthy to get into a "heated discussion" occasionally, but it can also provide opportunities for growth, understanding, and deeper connection. That is if it all stays within a certain level of respect.

Now if your heated discussion can flare up into something more, you are in the right place. Here is how you can not only get the most out of conflicts but also learn how to calm down when needed.

- **Identify Conflict Triggers:**

    Conflicts often stem from certain triconsiders that repeat themselves in relationships. These triggers can be rooted in past experiences, unmet needs, or differing perspectives.

    But how can you know, without communication, what the other person's triggers are? It's simple, start by understanding your own! What are the things that usually provoke you to be upset? What makes you sense angry, frustrated, or defensive? Once you better understand your own triggers, you can start to detect them in those around you.

    Did you notice that little magic word that we put in back there? Yup, you guessed it, "Communication." sometimes, guessing the other person's thoughts isn't a good idea, so talk to them. Know what sets them off.

    Now I might jump back and forth, but bear with me. You might think, "Okay, I must figure out my triggers first. But how would I know if something is a trigger until I'm already knee-deep in an argument?"

Well, just pay attention to your body! When you're feeling triggered, your body usually provides you with hints. You might start to tense up, your heartbeat could elevate, or you may experience nervousness in your gut. Pay attention to these physical changes, and they can aid you in determining your triggers.

Certain situations or environments can also cause conflict. For example, if you're always getting into arguments with your partner at the end of a long day, it may be caused by you both experiencing anxiousness and being exhausted. Once you're aware of the triggers in your environment, you can initiate avoiding them or discover methods to handle them.

- **Effective Communication During Conflict:**

We all have those days when things can, and very surprisingly at that, get out of hand. I know I've had my fair share. So when, and not if, conflicts arise, effective communication becomes even more crucial.

You must approach these situations with an open mind, respect, and a genuine willingness to understand each other's perspectives. And lucky for you, you now have just the tool for the job. Active listening! Pay attention to what the other person is saying not only with their mouth but with their body too. Try to understand what the other person's pain points are.

And when it's finally your turn to speak your truths, use "I" statements. This implies communicating your emotions and requirements by not criticizing the other person. For instance, instead of expressing, "You repeatedly make me doubt my worthiness," you may say, "I experience feelings of insecurity when you compare with others." You create a safe space for open dialogue by taking ownership of your emotions.

All these can help deflate the situation and facilitate a more productive conversation where you both learn and trust each other more, resulting in a more secure attachment.

- **Collaborative Problem-Solving:**

    Now we are getting to the end! Resolving conflicts isn't about one person winning or the other losing. It's about finding win-win solutions that address the underlying issues. It's about finding a solution through the means of teamwork.

    A study by the University of Michigan found that collaborative problem-solving can improve critical thinking and problem-solving skills.

    When detecting to attachment, working together to solve problems may be perceived as secure attachment.

    Insecure attachment, however, may make it more difficult for specific individuals to overcome difficulties in collaborative problem-solving. For instance, those with an anxious attachment may worry that their spouse won't be able to meet their needs, and they may also have excessive neediness or demanding tendencies. Or people with avoidant attachments may find it challenging to convey their feelings and mental "states," and they may put off trying to discover answers.

However, this isn't to say that people with insecure attachments can't improve their ability to work together to solve difficulties. They may cultivate a more profound connection by learning to express their needs and feelings clearly and having faith that their significant other will listen and support them.

It's essential to be aware of your attachment style as this may aid in your understanding of how you tend to respond in contentious conditions. And always think about the other person, too; listen actively, be respectful, be willing to compromise, and always remember to tune in to the problem, not the person.

Practical Exercises for Improving Relationship Skills

Now that we've handed you all the tools needed to become an expert in communication now's the time for you to practice because without practice, there's no getting it right. So without further ado, let's dive in!

- **Emotional Awareness Exercises**

    The Feelings Wheel: The Feelings Wheel, created by Dr. Gloria Willcox, is a simple yet effective tool for identifying and classifying feelings. It can help us when we are unsure of our feelings and require clarification for ourselves or another. You may even learn about a new emotion or two as a side benefit. Keep a screenshot of it on your phone or a small printout in your journal, and you can easily reference it whenever necessary.

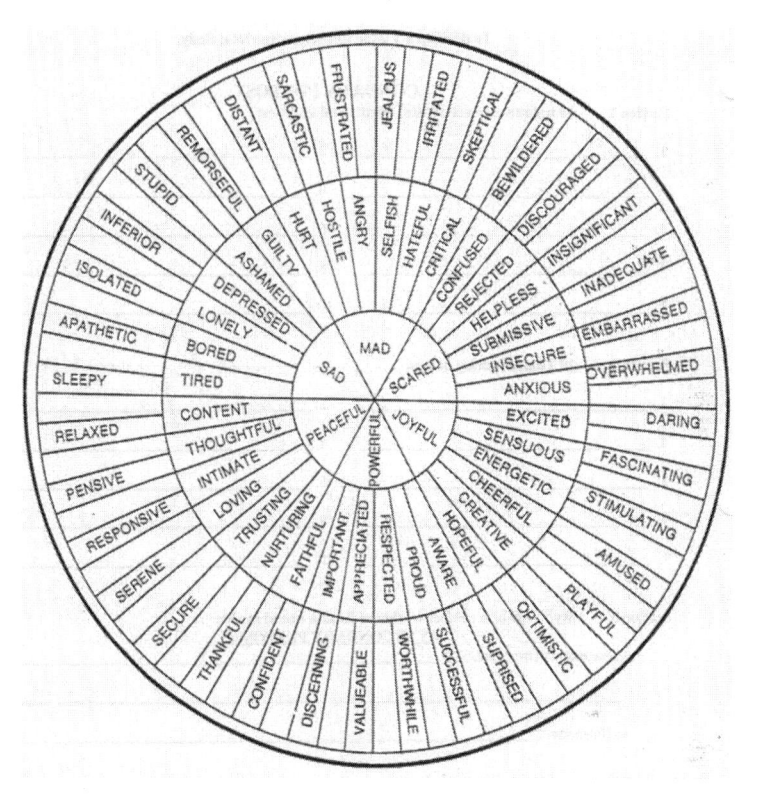

(Source: visualcapitalist.com)

The 5-Minute Journal: This is a meditation routine that helps you focus on the helpful components of your everyday encounters and personal exchanges. Each day, you write down three elements you admire, three accomplishments, and one fresh insight you obtained. This not only helps you put into perspective the positives that you encountered throughout the day but also helps you practice your communication skills.

- **Conflict Role-Play**

    Conflict is a crucial element amongst all connections. However, your skill in resolving conflicts can profoundly affect the robustness and stability of your relationship. An enjoyable way to build these skills is to get into an imaginary conflict with someone. But here's the kicker, you act as the other person, and they act as you. You switch roles! This can help you consider how you come across to the other person.

    These hands-on activities bring bonding theory to life, offering actual situations to implement its ideas. Keep in mind, development is by practicing and introspection. Welcome the adventure of personal growth and discovery, and be open to the revolutionary impact of these exercises in boosting your relational expertise.

Key Points:

- Effective communication strategies are essential for building secure attachments and fostering healthy relationships.

- Communication is not limited to words alone; nonverbal cues significantly convey meaning and understanding.

- Active listening is a powerful skill that promotes deeper connections and understanding between partners.

- Emotional awareness exercises help individuals recognize and express their emotions within the relationship.

- Building healthy boundaries through assertive expression fosters respect and emotional well-being.

- Conflict is a natural part of relationships, and effective conflict resolution is crucial for maintaining healthier dynamics.

- Identifying common conflict triggers and patterns helps gain insight into the underlying causes of conflicts.

- Effective communication during conflict involves using "I" statements, active listening, and empathy.

- Collaborative problem-solving techniques, such as compromise and negotiation, can lead to win-win solutions.

- Practical exercises, including emotional awareness exercises, relationship-building activities, and conflict role-plays, provide opportunities for hands-on growth and skill development opportunities.

- Practicing these exercises cultivates self-awareness, deepens connections, and fosters healthier communication and conflict resolution.

- Growth in relationship skills requires patience, practice, and a commitment to ongoing improvement.

Cultivating Growth and Transformation

"The only way to do great work is to love what you do." - Steve Jobs

Now, I know that attachment theory can be a complex topic. Still, it is also very empowering. And every bit that you learn about can go a long way. And hey, there's only so many bits left. In fact, this is your last step in becoming a better version of yourself.

This chapter will discuss embracing personal growth and development, developing long-term strategies for maintaining healthy attachments and integrating newfound knowledge into everyday life. So put your hats on, and let's get this boat (or ship) going.

Embracing Personal Growth and Development Through Attachment Transformation

So you might be thinking, what is attachment conversion, and why is it essential? As simple as it sounds, it alters your attachment style from insecure to secure or less secure to secure. Now, I'm confident that you are familiar with it all by now, but if you need a recap - Your attachment style is how you establish relationships and engage with individuals.

If you have an insecure attachment style, you may struggle with low self-esteem, suspicion, avoidance of closeness, or instability. You may also experience difficulties in your relationships, such as experiencing anxious emotions, clingy, disengaged, or emotionally distant. These relationship uncertainties and barriers can hinder your self-improvement and advancement and impede your progress toward achieving your maximum potential.

However, the bright is that your type is not forever. It can evolve according to your experiences and readiness to learn and improve. Change in attachment is possible for everyone who aims to improve the safety of their emotional bond and general welfare. By undergoing emotional maturation, you can overcome your attachment anxieties and develop a more positive outlook on yourself and others. You can also experience more satisfying and equitable relationships and greater happiness and success.

Now all this begs the question - How can you obtain attachment change?

Determine your attachment style! The first step to attachment transformation is knowing what yours is now. You might already know where you stand by now, but if you really need to put your mind at ease, you can explore books, blogs, or electronic journals on the topic or take online quizzes or tests to find your attachment style. Each person has unique skills, imperfections, specific behavioral traits, and knowledge sharing. By understanding your bonding style, you can acknowledge your bonding needs, worries, and stimuli and how they impact your life.

Now think about your attachment experiences and incidents and how they shaped your attachment style. Journaling while thinking about your past is a perfect way to do this. You can ask yourself questions such as: How was the bond with your guardians or caretakers while you were maturing? What was your reaction as you expressed your desires and emotions? How did they depict romantic bonds? How method did the initial romantic involvements impact your subsequent connections? How did you handle separation, mourning, or anguish? How did you share or suppress your sentiments? And so much more! You can gain more self-consciousness and relationship tendencies by reflecting on your relationship history and interactions.

The final phase of attachment transformation challenges your doubtful convictions and expectations stemming from your unstable bonding. You can do this by identifying the cognitive distortions or irrational thoughts that affect your self-image and your relationships, such as I lack competence; I'm unlovable; I must be flawless to be liked; I have trust issues; I must rely on myself; I need to keep my distance from others; I must always make everyone happy; I must have complete control; etc. This is where you can talk to your inner critic!

You can then replace these negative beliefs and expectations with more realistic and positive ones, such as I deserve love and respect; I can meet someone who accepts me as I am; I can embrace my imperfections; I can have faith in reliable individuals; I can rely on supportive individuals; I can experience closeness without sacrificing my identity; I can define healthy limits; I can release control over things beyond my power; etc. You can change your mindset and attitude toward yourself and others by challenging your negative beliefs and expectations.

The fourth step to bonding change is to adopt novel habits and abilities that will help you develop a more strong attachment approach. You can do this by putting yourself in unfamiliar circumstances and activities that will push your boundaries and widen your worldview.

You can also learn new skills to enhance your emotional intelligence and communication skills, such as self-love, awareness, appreciation, compassion, self-assurance, attentive listening, constructive criticism, dispute resolution, critical thinking, etc. By practicing new behaviors and skills, you can improve your proficiency and confidence in yourself and your interactions.

Great Job getting this far! But what's the benefit of all this?

Imagine how your life would be different if you felt relaxed with yourself and bold in being authentic. If you could acknowledge your strengths and limitations and celebrate your individuality. If you could manage your sentiments in beneficial and practical approaches. If you could deal with stress and worry more efficiently. If you could deal with conflict and constructive criticism more composedly and politely. If you could express your requirements and emotions more transparently and sincerely. And the list can go on and on.

All these favorable changes are possible if you experience attachment transformation. Changing your attachment style from insecure to secure can improve your confidence, connections, and happiness. You can create more satisfying and deep relationships with yourself and others. And you can attain greater joy and accomplishment in your existence.

These are some tips and exercises for cultivating a growth mindset and a secure attachment style:

Cultivating Growth and Transformation

One of the keys to attachment transformation is to nurture a belief in personal development. A growth mindset entails the idea that you can transform, educate yourself, and expand. It contradicts a faxed attitude, which is the perspective that you are confined to your identity, possessions, and potential.

A growth mindset can empower you to adopt self-improvement and progress through a mindset shift. It can support you in viewing challenges as chances instead of threats. This can aid in recognizing errors as constructive criticism instead of a setback. Which can then assist in identifying shift as confident, not intimidating.

How can you develop a growth mindset? Here are some tips and exercises that can help:

- Adopt a curious and open-minded attitude toward learning and growing! Instead of avoiding or resisting new situations or experiences, seek them out and explore them. Instead of shutting down or giving up when faced with difficulties or setbacks, keep trying and experimenting. Instead of saying "I can't" or "I don't know," say "I can" or "I'll find out."

- Seek feedback from others who can help you improve. Have no fear of their viewpoints, ideas, or guidance. Don't criticize personally or defensively, especially if it is constructive. You know, actionable stuff that you can use to improve. Alternatively, become open to their suggestions and acquire knowledge from their outlooks, knowledge, or proficiency

- Acknowledge how far you've come! Regardless of how far it is. Don't ignore or belittle your dedication, advancement, or achievements. Instead, recognize them and incentivize yourself with something that brings you joy. And don't hold back your accomplishments to yourself only, also. Spread the word among friends who value you and party with them.

- Look for mentors that motivate you. Locate individuals who have succeeded in your desired outcome or conquered your challenges. Gain knowledge from the narratives of approaches or recommendations. Imitate their actions, practices, or attitudes.

- Envelop yourself with optimistic and helpful companions. Discover individuals that have your beliefs, passions, or targets. Engage with individuals who uplift, drive, or test you personally. Steer clear of individuals who exhaust, dissuade, or sabotage you.

- Be kind to yourself with compassion, empathy, and pardon. Don't criticize yourself critically or differentiate yourself poorly from others. Don't dwell on your flaws or sorrow. Pay attention to your abilities and potentialities.

By following these tips and exercises, you can cultivate a growth mindset and a secure attachment style. You can become more open, flexible, and resilient in the face of change and challenge. You can become more confident, happy, and fulfilled in yourself and your relationships.

Long-Term Strategies for Maintaining Healthy Attachments

Attachment transformation is not a one-time event but a lifelong journey. It requires ongoing effort, practice, and commitment to sustain healthy attachments. For many people, this is where things start to go downhill, where that initial burst of motivation dies down. Leaving them stuck in a place of comfortable complacency. But lucky for you, you are not alone. Here are some long-term strategies that can help you maintain healthy attachments in the long run.

- **Self-awareness**

    Self-awareness is the ability to recognize and understand your thoughts, feelings, and behaviors and how they affect yourself and others. Self-awareness is essential for maintaining healthy attachments because it helps you:

    - Identify your attachment style, needs, fears, and triggers
    - Monitor your attachment patterns and habits
    - Evaluate your attachment strengths and weaknesses
    - Adjust your attachment expectations and goals
    - Learn from your attachment experiences and feedback

    Doesn't that sound amazing? And don't even worry about keeping a constant internal eye on yourself at the start. There are many tips and tricks to help you develop this ability almost effortlessly.

    - Keep a journal of your attachment thoughts, feelings, and behaviors. Write down what you think, feel, and do about yourself and others. Note any patterns, themes, or insights that emerge.
    - Ask for feedback from others who know you well. Ask them how they perceive you, what they appreciate

about you, what they find challenging about you, and what they suggest for you to improve.

- Meditate or practice mindfulness. These practices can help you become more aware of your present-moment experience without judgment or distraction. They can also help you calm your mind and body and reduce stress and anxiety.

- Communication

As always, the importance of communication can never be understated. There's not a lot that we haven't already gone over before. So here's cutting all the fluff and letting you in on another little secret to help you become a communication master.

Feedback refers to providing or receiving positive critique or appreciation for someone's work or conduct. This can aid in enhancing individual skills or bonds when done correctly. To give feedback effectively, use the sandwich method: commence with praise, identify improvement areas, and conclude with a compliment. On the other hand, to receive feedback effectively, use the STAR method: be attentive (Stop), show appreciation (Thank), request further information (Ask), and offer a positive response (Respond).

- **Emotional regulation**

Emotion control refers to efficiently controlling and regulating personal feelings to preserve emotional wellness and overcome life's difficulties in a well-rounded and stable fashion. It encompasses the skill to perceive, grasp and suitably handle various emotions, irrespective of their positive or negative nature.

Emotion regulation involves multiple processes and approaches that assist individuals in regulating and managing their emotional responses. It involves having knowledge of one's emotions, grasping the fundamental causes and triggers, and selecting the manner of expressing and responding to them in a beneficial approach. All of this can help you, Cope with attachment triggers, stressors, and conflicts, Prevent emotional overreactions or underreactions, Avoid emotional avoidance or suppression, and help you become stronger!

Here are some tips and exercises to help you develop this skill:

Identify your emotions and their causes. Name what you are feeling and why you are feeling it. For example, "I feel angry because he lied to me." This can help you understand your emotions better and reduce their intensity.

Choose healthy coping strategies for your emotions. Depending on the situation and the feeling, you can choose different coping strategies, such as: breathing deeply, counting to ten, taking a break, distracting yourself, talking to someone, writing it down, etc. These strategies can help you calm down and regain control of your emotions.

Challenge negative or irrational thoughts that fuel your emotions. Sometimes, your feelings are influenced by distorted or unrealistic ideas, such as: "I'm worthless," "Everyone hates me," "It's all my fault," "Nothing will ever change," etc. These thoughts can make you feel worse and affect your behavior.

You can challenge these thoughts by asking yourself questions, such as: "Is this true?", "Is this helpful?", "Is there another way to look at this?", "What would I tell a friend in this situation?" etc. These questions can help you replace negative or irrational thoughts with more positive or realistic ones.

Express your emotions in healthy and constructive ways. Don't bottle up or ignore your emotions, leading to more problems later. Don't lash out or act on your emotions; this can hurt yourself or others. Instead, express your feelings in healthy and constructive ways, such as: crying, laughing, singing, dancing, painting, etc. These ways can help you release your emotions and feel better.

- **Coping with attachment triggers**

    These are some ways to cope with attachment triggers, stressors, and conflicts in constructive and respectful ways:

    Identify your attachment triggers, stressors, and conflicts. These situations or events make you feel insecure, anxious, angry, or sad concerning your attachment style. For example, if you have an anxious attachment style, you may feel triggered by your partner's lack of attention, affection, or reassurance. If you have an avoidant attachment style, you may feel stressed by your partner's demands, expectations, or emotions. If you have a fearful-avoidant attachment style, you may feel conflicted by your partner's closeness or distance. By identifying attachment triggers, stressors, and conflicts, you can prepare for them and plan how to deal with them.

    Nurture: Nurture yourself and others with kindness and care. What can you do to help yourself or others in this situation? How can you meet your needs and wants in this situation? How can you express your feelings and thoughts in this situation?

Use the DEAR MAN technique: DEAR MAN is a simple but powerful acronym that stands for all the different things you can do to express yourself clearly and confidently in any situation. Whether you want to ask for a favor, say no, or want to resolve a conflict, this is the tool for the job.

Here's what it stands for:

- **D**escribe: Explain the situation. No need to add any interpretation yet. Just simply describe it how it is. For, e.g., "I have been working here for two years and consistently met or exceeded my targets."

- **E**xpress: Share your feelings and opinions using "I" statements. An example could be, "I feel that I have contributed a lot to the company, and I enjoy working here."

- **A**ssert: Be assertive! (Im sure you already knew this part). Ask for what you want or say no clearly and respectfully. For e.g., "I would like to request a 10% raise in my salary."

- **R**einforce: Explain the benefits of getting what you want or the consequences of not getting it. For e.g., "This would reflect my performance and value to the company and motivate me to continue working hard."

- **M**indful: Stay focused on your goal and beat around the bush. For, e.g., "I understand that this is a difficult time for the company, but I hope you can consider my request."

- **A**ppear confident: Use confident body language, eye contact, tone of voice, and words. - Maintain eye contact, speak clearly and firmly, and avoid fidgeting or apologizing.

- **N**egotiate: Be willing to compromise and find a win-win solution. For, e.g., "If 10% is not possible right now, maybe we can agree on a lower percentage or a future date for the raise."

Tools for Integrating Newfound Knowledge into Everyday Life

In the previous sections, we have learned a lot about attachment theory and how it can help us grow and transform as individuals and partners. We've also reviewed the different attachment styles and how they affect our self-esteem, relationships, and well-being. We have learned about the process of attachment transformation and how it can help us overcome our attachment insecurities and challenges. We have learned about the long-term strategies for maintaining healthy attachments and how they can help us cope with attachment triggers, stressors, and conflicts.

But learning is not enough. We also need to apply what we have learned to our everyday life. We must integrate our newfound knowledge, experiment with different attachment strategies, and determine how this could work for you. It may not sound simple initially, but we must make attachment theory a part of our lifestyle!

Now bear with me a little longer; there isn't much left. But before I get into it, I just want to point out that I'm so proud of you. You've done an excellent job in making it this far, and I sincerely hope you can stay on this past to becoming the best/emotionally intelligent person you can be.

After finishing everything, examine the main ideas and the principles that govern attachment theory and their practical implications in diverse contexts and situations. Attachment theory is relevant for intimate and other relationships, such as relatives, companions, coworkers, etc.

Reviewing the main ideas and principles of bonding theory, we can reiterate what we have gained and how we can utilize it in diverse environments and situations. For instance, we can examine the four attachment styles and their impact on our interaction, reliance, closeness, and resolving conflicts in diverse relationship dynamics. We can also examine the stages of attachment transformation and how they can help us enhance our self-knowledge, interaction, mood management, and progress mindset in diverse dimensions of our being.

Some instruments and approaches can help us apply attachment theory to our personal and career. Some examples are

The Attachment Style Quiz: This is a simple online quiz developed by Amir Levine and Rachel Heller in 2015. It can help you understand your attachment style and its strengths and weaknesses. Now I know that doing a quiz can sound daunting for some of you, but don't worry. It will only take 10 minutes, and you can easily find it online by going to "attachedthebook.com"

The Attachment Style Wheel:

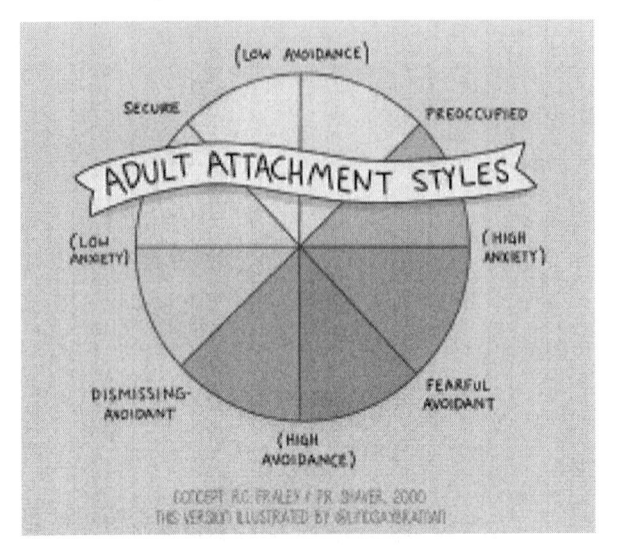

(Source: LindsayBraman.com)

This visual aid can help us outline our emotional connection style and its aspects. It consists of a circle divided into four quadrants, each representing one of the four attachment styles: confident, worried, detached, or fearful. We can use this instrument to graph and compare and contrast our bonding style. Additionally, we can utilize the tool to detect opportunities for growth or objectives for our relationship modification.

The Attachment Style Journal: Back to Journaling! All you need to do for this one is to ask yourself a few questions. Some examples of queries are: What is your emotional response when you are near somebody? What is it you sense when you feel separated from someone? How do you manage your sentiments in your connections? How do you articulate your needs and ideas in your relationships? How do you manage disagreement or constructive criticism in your relations? How do you follow your aspirations or desires in your interactions? We can utilize this tool to note our responses regularly and examine any trends or observations that arise.

Now I hope this all motivated you to go and figure yourself out! And not only just understand but also implement all the various strategies we've discussed to help you get going and become the best version of yourself.

By experimenting with different attachment strategies and tracking our progress and outcomes, we can see what works for us and what doesn't. We can also see how we change and grow as people and partners. We can also see how our relationships are improving and flourishing.

Key Takeaways:

- Cultivating growth and transformation through attachment theory is lifelong.

- There are many strategies that we can use to maintain healthy attachments.

- It is essential to integrate newfound knowledge about attachment theory into our everyday life.

Action Steps:

- Seek therapy or counseling if you need additional support.

- Pay attention to your thoughts, feelings, and behaviors in your relationships.

- Keep a journal to track your progress and reflect on your learning.

- Talk to your partners about what you are learning.

Conclusion

"All hurt is founded on attachment to anything regardless of its nature. When we detach we vibrationally send ourselves back into the flow of life."
— Dr. Jacinta Mpalyenkana, Ph.D, MBA

I will end this book with this quote. We have learned repeatedly that the wounds we get during childhood stick with us and impact our lives as adults. We have also heard the phrase "Hurt people hurt people" over and over again, and as sad as it may be, it proves to be true even today. With this book, I hope to leave you less hurt and more hope. The ideas presented within these pages show that if left untreated, wounds hurt us and those around us. But I haven't left you to fend for yourself. There are multitudes of ways to find peace within yourself and make it so that you come to terms with your past and change your attachment style to something more secure.

If you've reached this far, I'm sure we agree to some things, if not all. I hope this book wasn't just an information dump but a little journey we took together. This book covers everything from learning attachment theory to recognizing different attachment styles, understanding which type we belong to, and figuring out how to change and adapt.

We talked about how attachment styles can influence our relationships and how we interact with the world around us. We looked into several tips and tricks that you can easily use to transform your attachment style. From Somatic Experiencing to meditation, from R.A.I.N technique to the DEARMAN technique, I've got your back. I hope this book will help you understand yourself more deeply and improve your interpersonal relationships.

The techniques I have mentioned also enable you to construct solid arguments that will help you understand your past and progress in the present, which is the most important thing you can do to live a life free of the most detrimental impositions of your past. Making sense of your past and experiencing the depth of your childhood trauma are necessary steps in this process. Then and only then can you start changing your perspective on the world or your interpersonal relationships.

You have the power to modify your relationships to be what you want them to be rather than unknowingly reliving your upbringing and reformulating identical relationships to those you had when you were a child. A strong, safe relationship will significantly transform your attachment style because you will have direct contact with a trustworthy, considerate, and sensitive partner. Instead of adopting the viewpoint of your critical inner voice, you may perceive the world more realistically. You can create better relationships and lead the life you want, not the one dictated to you by your past.

The best strategy to develop stable attachment would undoubtedly be to work on this pattern with a therapist. But For you to continue advancing, I am providing this book. Either way, you must work hard to change your attachment style. Persistence and effort are crucial whether you are working through it with a close friend, a therapist, or a book.

And throughout the past many years of working on myself in this area, I can tell you from my own experiences that I've noticed myself move from a strong-anxious attachment style to

Conclusion

a more secure attachment. And I am confident to let you all know that my relationships with people around me have made me happier and more satisfied.

I will leave you with this: It is nearly impossible to put humans into boxes, but we can find common ground and categorize ourselves as leaning towards one thing on the other. In this case, understanding which attachment style we tend to lean towards can drastically improve us. But if you find yourself in a predicament thinking you don't have the attachment style you had wished for, don't fret. Human beings are not rigid in their ways. Our minds are malleable, and we change and adapt throughout our lives. All I can say is to try to be the most authentic and earnest version of yourself and seek to improve your relationships daily. If you're doing that, you've already reached your goals.

Thank You

Thank you so much for purchasing my book.

There were dozens of options, but you took a chance on this book.

Thank you for taking this journey with me and making it all the way to the end.

Before you go, allow me to ask for a tiny favour. Would you please consider posting a review on the platform? It only takes 5 seconds.

Posting a review is the best and easiest way to support the work of independent authors like me.

Your feedback will help me keep writing and sharing the books and resources to propel you towards your desired results.

Hearing from you would mean the world.

https://www.amazon.com/review/create-review

References

A, S. M. L., Herrington, A., & Henderson, L. M. (2011). 10: Defining critical thinking in higher education. *To Improve the Academy*, *30*(20210331). https://doi.org/10.3998/tia.17063888.0030.014

Andersen, T. E., Lahav, Y., Ellegaard, H., & Manniche, C. (2017). A randomized controlled trial of brief Somatic Experiencing for chronic low back pain and comorbid post-traumatic stress disorder symptoms. *European Journal of Psychotraumatology*, *8*(1). https://doi.org/10.1080/20008198.2017.1331108

Bai, Y., Kong, F., Wang, Y., & Zhang, Y. (n.d.). Efficacy of expressive writing for anxiety: A systematic review and meta-analysis. *Journal of Affective Disorders*, *234*, 321–329. https://doi.org/10.1016/j.jad.2018.01.040

Bodie, G. D., & McDonald, P. (2009). The relationship between active listening and leadership effectiveness: A study of hospital managers. *Journal of Health Organization and Management*, *23*(1), 50–65. https://doi.org/10.1108/14777260910925838

Carnegie, D. A. (1936). *How to win friends & influence people*. http://ci.nii.ac.jp/ncid/BB02478846?l=en

Covey, S., & Blankenhagen, D. (1991). The 7 habits of highly effective people. *Performance + Instruction*, *30*(10), 38. https://doi.org/10.1002/pfi.4170301009

Creswell, J. D., Welch, T. R., & Sherman, D. K. (2017). Affirming positive qualities can improve cognitive abilities: A randomized controlled trial of the self-affirmation effect. *Journal of Positive Psychology*, *12*(2), 158–166. https://doi.org/10.1080/17439760.2017.1288134

Cummings, G. G., MacGregor, T., Davey, M., Lee, H. S., Wong, C. A., Lo, E., Muise, M., & Stafford, E. (2010). Leadership styles and outcome patterns for the nursing workforce and work environment: A systematic review. *International Journal of Nursing Studies, 47*(3), 363–385. https://doi.org/10.1016/j.ijnurstu.2009.08.006

Effa, C. (2022, December 6). *How can you fix an anxious attachment style?* https://www.medicalnewstoday.com/articles/how-to-fix-anxious-attachment-style

G. Maunder, R., & J. Hunter, J. (n.d.). Attachment style, avoidance of negative emotions, and inflammatory response to stress. *Journal of Psychosomatic Medicine, 53*(5), 737–745. https://doi.org/10.1016/s0033-2917(01)00179-4

Gillath, O., Selcuk, E., & Shaver, P. R. (2017). Anxious-preoccupied attachment and couple functioning: Longitudinal findings from a community sample. *Social Psychological and Personality Science, 8*(6), 677–685. https://doi.org/10.1177/1948550617709255

Harms, P., Mavroveli, S., & A. Coan, J. (n.d.). Secure attachment and resilience: A prospective study of stress reactivity and recovery. *Personality and Social Psychology Bulletin, 44*(1), 20–33. https://doi.org/10.1177/0146167217744153

Kabat-Zinn, J., Massion, A. O., Kristeller, J. L., Peterson, L. R., Fletcher, K. E., Pbert, L., Lenderking, W. R., & Santorelli, S. F. (1992). Effectiveness of a meditation-based stress reduction program in the treatment of anxiety disorders. *American Journal of Psychiatry, 149*(7), 936–943. https://doi.org/10.1176/ajp.149.7.936

Kruuk, H., & Hinde, R. A. (1973). Non-verbal communication. *Journal of Animal Ecology, 42*(1), 208. https://doi.org/10.2307/3423

References

Nummenmaa, L., Glerean, E., Hari, R., & Hietanen, J. K. (2013). Bodily maps of emotions. *Proceedings of the National Academy of Sciences*, *111*(2), 646–651. https://doi.org/10.1073/pnas.1321664111

Peters, E., & Bjälkebring, P. (2015). Multiple numeric competencies: When a number is not just a number. *Journal of Personality and Social Psychology*, *108*(5), 802–822. https://doi.org/10.1037/pspp0000019

Price, C. J., & Weng, H. Y. (2021). Facilitating adaptive emotion processing and somatic reappraisal via sustained mindful interoceptive attention. *Frontiers in Psychology*, *12*. https://doi.org/10.3389/fpsyg.2021.578827

Team. (2023, April 6). *Attachment styles and their role in adult relationships*. Attachment Project. https://www.attachmentproject.com/blog/four-attachment-styles/

Xu, S., Baker, D., & Ren, F. (2021). The positive role of Tai Chi in responding to the COVId-19 pandemic. *International Journal of Environmental Research and Public Health*, *18*(14), 7479. https://doi.org/10.3390/ijerph18147479

Printed in Poland
by Amazon Fulfillment
Poland Sp. z o.o., Wrocław